W9-AVT-389

MOSCOW

MEETS

MADISON

AVENUE

MOSCOW MEETS MADISON AVENUE

THE ADVENTURES OF THE FIRST AMERICAN ADMAN IN THE U.S.S.R.

GARY BURANDT
WITH NANCY GIGES

 HarperBusiness
A Division of HarperCollinsPublishers

HarperCollins books may be purchased for educational, business, or sales promotional use. For information, please write: Special Markets Department, HarperCollins Publishers, Inc., 10 East 53rd Street, New York, NY 10022.

FIRST EDITION

Designed by Claudyne Bianco

Library of Congress Cataloging-in-Publication Data

Burandt, Gary.
    Moscow meets Madison Avenue : the adventures of the first American adman in the U.S.S.R. / Gary Burandt, Nancy Giges.
        p. cm.
    ISBN 0-88730-570-9 (cloth)
    1. Burandt, Gary. 2. Advertising executives—Russian S.F.S.R.—Moscow—Biography. 3. Advertising agencies—Russian S.F.S.R.—Moscow. 4. Young & Rubicam (Moscow, R.S.F.S.R.) I. Giges, Nancy. II. Title.
HF5810.B87A3   1992
659.1' 092—dc20
[B]   92-52609

92 93 94 95 96 ❖/HC 10 9 8 7 6 5 4 3 2 1

This book is dedicated to my mother and father,
who started my trip to Moscow in
Kansas City by teaching hard work with love
—GARY BURANDT

and to my mother, Leah, whose love
and devotion have inspired me to
make dreams come true
—NANCY GIGES

CONTENTS

Photographs follow page 112

INTRODUCTION

THIS STORY IS TRUE TO THE BEST OF MY MEMORY. THOUGH I MUST admit that a story about starting an ad agency in the Soviet Union surely would have been fiction not too many years ago.

It is my story, told with the faithful and patient help of Nancy Giges, international editor of *Advertising Age*. It was Nancy who conducted the first interview with me after my first trip to Moscow. It was Nancy who suggested, "There may be a book there." To that end, I kept a journal of events—usually written early in the morning. Unfortunately, the days with the best stories often ended with too much drink, fogging the memory and hampering sunrise journal entries.

When I returned from Moscow, Nancy and I met many Sunday mornings to put together this book. She had read my journals and developed questions about various subjects. Over coffee and bagels I would answer the questions into her tape recorder. As a result, this book is constructed topically not chronologically. Each chapter stands alone examining a topic, theme, or person.

This is also the story of many other people, mostly American and Soviet, who played major roles in conceiving, financing, supporting, and building the first advertising agency in the "workers' paradise."

A lot has been written about advertising and how to create it. This story also is about advertising; but unlike others, it starts long before the first clients sign up, and even before the agency name is on the door.

It starts with creating an environment to encourage the freethinking that precedes good ideas, smart strategies, and exciting ad campaigns. It starts with finding the best people for the job and finding a place for them to work productively. Most important, it starts with teaching the concept of choice—free choice in a free marketplace.

If this all sounds boring, it may well have been so had this story taken place almost anywhere else. But my assignment was in a country where choice is a new concept, where store shelves are almost always bare. The Soviet Union.

I could describe this book as "One Man's Frustrations Against an Illogical, Reprehensible System"—a system that imposed suspicion and bureaucracy upon common Western business practices. But this is not a book about politics. It is about bringing a new way of business to good people trapped in a bad system.

I was thrown back in time, working under conditions of a much earlier decade when advertising was considered pure hucksterism. Yet I know that my chosen profession has become an important factor in making the United States a leader in business and trade. I have no doubts whatsoever about advertising's respectability, responsibility, and its role as a sophisticated communication tool.

I had tackled tough assignments before: Launching Spain's SEAT car across Europe in 1983; introducing Unisys around the world in sixty days when the name wasn't known until two days before the launch date; driving a minesweeper in the mouth of the Mekong River. However, nothing I had done previously compares to the combination of professional and personal frustrations and rewards of the Moscow job.

Simply put, advertising in a free market stimulates the development and sale of better goods and services. It benefits people, business, and society—by helping to raise the standard of living and improving the quality of life. It's not a perfect tool by any means, nor problem free. And yes, it can be and has been used improperly. But advertising is a key element in the best economic system yet devised by modern men and women.

I chose advertising as a career in college because it seemed an interesting combination of creative arts and business science. I have a bachelor of journalism degree with an emphasis in advertising from the University of Missouri, and I have practiced advertising since graduation in 1966, except for a tour as a naval officer in Vietnam. Since 1972, I have worked for a large international advertising agency, Young & Rubicam.

I knew Moscow would be different from my other international postings, but I couldn't imagine how different until I actually arrived. I quickly realized I was trying to open an ad agency in a country where an important means of trade still is basic barter. ("I'll trade my mittens for your six slabs of soap.") This is a city where people will stand in line forty-five minutes for a handout of a tiny free sample tube of toothpaste because usually they stand in line for hours just for the privilege of *buying* toothpaste. This is a city where the notion of the branded product was nonexistent, and the concept of choice—in the marketplace or in politics—virtually unknown.

It's no wonder people threw strange looks and comments my way whenever I explained that I was in the Soviet Union to open the first ad agency. In developing and underdeveloped economies, where basic goods—food, personal care items, and clothing—are in short supply, people don't need to be persuaded to buy. This was the environment I entered in 1988 to set up a modern ad agency. With all this against me, the most logical question to ask is why?

And the answer is simple. If Young & Rubicam clients, mostly major American corporations such as Johnson & Johnson, General Electric, Du Pont, and Colgate-Palmolive, were entering the new Soviet Union of *glasnost* and *perestroika* and saw it as a land of opportunity—and they did—then we had to be there, too. Being first also gave us the advantage of having a headstart on our competition.

In theory, the Soviets were ready. Mikhail Gorbachev, in laying out his broad-based plan to lead his country into the twenty-first century, recognized that the nation was on the brink of economic and social disaster. "Enterprises must be put in such conditions as to encourage competition for the best satisfaction of consumer demands, and employees' incomes must strictly depend on end product results, on profits," he wrote in his famous *Perestroika*. Gorbachev recognized the importance of providing his people with food, consumer goods, adequate housing, and health care, as well as more fully meeting their basic needs.

I believe he realized that the great social experiment of the last seventy years had failed. There was no place on the planet where communism was providing a decent lifestyle. In order for the Soviet people to catch up with Western standards, he had to introduce Western methods. Economically, this was an easy decision; politically, it took great courage. As events developed, the political changes proved easier than the economics.

Lenin had called advertising people the leeches of capitalism. As recently as the 1940s, the Soviet Encyclopedia couldn't have been more derogatory about advertising. Its definition: "swindling." But no more. The current definition is one that I could live with: "Advertising involves the popularization of goods with the aim of selling them, the creation of demand for these goods, the acquaintance of consumers with the quality, particular features, location of their sales and the explanation of the method of their use."

Yet, even Gorbachev's desire to move to a free market system couldn't immediately wipe out the well-entrenched bureaucratic practices, nor erase the suspicion of capitalist business practices passed down from generation to generation.

This is what this book is about. It's not a list of do's, don'ts, and how-to's, although I hope others opening a service business in the former Soviet Union—either on their own or as a joint venture—can benefit from these experiences. Advertising is my business, but virtually any service business will surely face similar "challenges." On the other hand, this is the story of one enterprise and the hardworking, adventuresome group of people who created it. So what worked for us may not work for others. In the four years since I embarked on my adventure, much has changed, not the least being the name and composition of what was the U.S.S.R. Since the country was known as the Soviet Union during the time I worked in Moscow, I have used its old name throughout this book.

Hopefully, the changes will make things easier for those who follow. This is the story of what life was like for me and my family, who put up with a tough lifestyle to allow me to do my job the best way I knew how.

I have tried to tell this story in an entertaining fashion, and if, in doing so, I've offended or embarrassed anyone, I apologize. Situations that I can now laugh about frustrated me greatly at the time. My rantings and ravings were not then or now aimed at particular individuals, but are directed at an inflexible system so ingrained that even those inside pushing for change often throw up their hands in despair.

The best part of the Soviet experience is the Soviet people. They are warm, intelligent, humorous, and incredibly generous with what little they have. Unfortunately, the path to a better life for them will be a tough one. I wish them well.

MOSCOW

MEETS

MADISON

AVENUE

1

HOW IT ALL STARTED

THE RAUCOUS JANGLING OF THE PHONE JOLTED ME OUT OF A DEEP sleep, and it rang out once more before I could find the receiver in the blackness.

"Hello," I mumbled, trying to inject some strength into my voice as I struggled to wake up. I listened to the apologies I had grown accustomed to from people calling me in the middle of the night in Moscow because they couldn't get a phone call through at any other time. (There were only twenty some phone lines connecting the United States with the U.S.S.R.) The apology gave me time to gather my thoughts and find the lamp switch.

The dim light thrown out by the bedside lamp reminded me that after several months of traveling back and forth to Moscow, I never could get used to the drab surroundings of these typical Moscow hotels that were becoming my home away from home.

I sat up straighter in bed to shake myself awake and think

what to say to the caller. It was someone from ABC, and she wanted Mike Adams and me to be guests on a network TV special that Ted Koppel was coming to Moscow to tape. The special was on the subject of television, and it would include a segment about the Soviet Union.

"Let me call you back tomorrow," I said. I wanted some time to think about whether we were ready to discuss the progress of Y&R/Sovero, the joint venture advertising agency we were starting, and I wanted to get Mike's opinion. He was my American partner in this adventure.

"You know, Mike," I said to him the next day, "we could use the publicity. I want the folks back home to know how far along we've come in achieving what a lot of people said was impossible."

"Do you think that outweighs any little secrets we might be giving away to competitors?" he asked.

"I do."

"Then let's go for it," he urged.

"Where do you think we should suggest for the interview?" We had just been assigned new office space after the first building we were renovating was taken away from us. The new office, not yet renovated, was a mess. A hotel didn't seem very businesslike, and ... "Just tell them what the office situation is. They'll have some ideas," Mike's wise suggestion interrupted my thoughts.

"That's probably the best thing to do," I agreed.

After I called back Koppel's people, I began to give a lot of thought to how much detail I wanted to get into in front of millions of Americans. Should I mention our brush with the KGB? Or the time Mike and I were able to slip into the U.S. Embassy unnoticed? Or Mike's disappearing toilet? They were all loosely related to getting into the ad business in Moscow. But maybe I should stick to the traditional discussion. On the other hand, nothing about the ad business in Moscow is traditional.

As I mulled over what I wanted to be prepared to say, I thought back to that day last September little more than nine months ago when I was in my office at Young & Rubicam in New York. It was a beautiful fall day in 1988 and I got a call from Mitch Kurz.

"Stand by for an important announcement tomorrow," he warned.

Mitch was first lieutenant to Alex Kroll, chairman/CEO of Young & Rubicam, and troubleshooter on special projects. "There's something you'll need to alert clients to. I'll be back to you tomorrow."

I thought perhaps there had been some sort of merger or a reshuffling of management. These were the kinds of changes that you normally tell clients about before they are announced so that they're aware of the news before they read it in the press. The past few years had been marked by merger and acquisition mania in the agency business, but I was pretty sure that was all behind us now.

At Y&R, we were especially sensitive when some change could be construed as bad news, so I was quite curious about what Mitch would tell me the next day. As the worldwide account director on Du Pont and Unisys, it was my job to make sure they were informed and understood the significance of any announcements.

By the next morning, I had imagined all sorts of things, from management shakeups to takeovers and more. Then Mitch told me, "Y&R has signed a letter of intent to create a joint venture advertising agency in Moscow."

"Terrific. That's going to be a great job for someone," I said.

"You really think so?"

"Sure. Imagine being the first Western adman in Moscow. How exciting. What a challenge!"

There was a pause, and then Mitch said, "Hold that thought. By the way, there's a press conference at four P.M. on the twenty-fifth floor if you're interested."

Alex Kroll; Jim Dowling, the CEO of Burson-Marsteller, Y&R's public relations company; John Cooper, Y&R's general counsel; and a couple of other senior managers had made the announcement in Moscow that morning. They got on a plane and were flying back to New York to make the same announcement that afternoon. The eight-hour time difference allowed the same execs to appear at the two press conferences in cities five thousand miles apart on the same day.

I couldn't stop thinking about my conversation with Mitch all day long. I went to the press conference that afternoon and sat fascinated by what the excited but weary executives were saying. I picked up a press kit for myself. All the way home on the commuter train I wondered if this job was something I should try for.

If you've lived internationally, as I have for half of my career, it gets in your blood. The challenge of starting something from scratch in a fascinating country was like a magnet. The U.S.S.R. under Mikhail Gorbachev was like Rip Van Winkle discovering what had happened while he had been asleep. The Russian people hadn't been asleep: they had been isolated from the outside world by a terribly closed and repressive political system. Under Gorbachev's policy of *glasnost* (openness) and *perestroika* (reconstruction), the Soviet Union was becoming a land of opportunity and, for me, adventure.

I wanted a job where I could make a difference. My family and I had been back from Paris for three years. I was getting restless with the routine of commuting into New York from

Connecticut, even though my job involved quite a bit of international travel.

I tested my wife Freddye's reaction at dinner. "What if we were to move to Moscow?"

Freddye was a Navy brat and used to moving frequently. We'd never lived in one place more than four years, and we both liked living abroad. I guess I had already concluded that I wanted to be the first Western adman in the Soviet Union. Freddye was usually game for any excitement and challenge, but as usual, she did much more thinking before stating her opinion and didn't jump to conclusions as quickly as I did. Our teenage daughters and their schooling were a major concern.

I had wanted to be the first Western adman in China when Y&R opened an office in Beijing in 1985. But at that time I had just transferred from Brussels to Paris for a new job, so the Beijing appointment was not a possibility for me.

"How do I get considered?" I asked Mitch the next day.

"Speak to Kroll. He's making this decision himself," he told me.

I felt I had a lot to offer: I had lived abroad. I had successfully run a small office before in Brussels. And I had been involved in business-to-business advertising, which initially would be much of what the Moscow office would be doing.

I made an appointment with Kroll and listed all my qualifications. "You'll certainly be considered," he told me, but he was noncommittal.

Colleagues and friends whose opinions I respect highly presented a bleak picture of life in Moscow and even tried to dissuade me. My old friend Joe DeDeo, who was then head of Y&R Europe, talked to me sternly over a beer.

"Do you *really* know what you're in for? Are you sure this is what you want?"

I admitted that I'd never been to Moscow, but I still wanted the job.

"It's an awful lifestyle," he told me. "The best hotel in town is like the worst hotel you've ever stayed in. The food is bad and the people are often afraid to be friendly. The language is difficult. The weather is awful." His warnings didn't change my mind.

For about a month, I didn't hear a word. Then one day Alex asked to meet with me during a trip to Bermuda, where I was making a presentation to the board of directors about the Du Pont account. He greeted me at the door to his hotel room with a big grin.

"You're our man in Moscow." Uncharacteristically, he showed his excitement. "You'll report directly to me." He outlined his vision: "The Moscow office will operate at the same high standard as we give our clients anywhere in the world. Our mission is to train as well as to do the work."

All sorts of unrelated thoughts began racing through my head. It was clear to me, though, that this job was going to either make or break my career, considering the extremely high visibility. It was also clear to me that this was a job Alex would have liked to have done himself.

He promised me his firm support and said another American, someone not yet selected from Burson-Marsteller, would be part of the U.S. team.

"This is not an assignment that one person can do alone," he said. "And we expect PR to be an important part of the services we will offer."

I felt I was on the brink of something very special. We shook hands and opened a couple of beers. He toasted our expected success. My elation completely destroyed any memory of the specifics of our conversation that afternoon.

I spent the evening with my colleagues also attending the

board meeting, who toasted my exciting adventure at dinner—with vodka. The next few weeks were filled with activity as word got out that I would be going to Moscow. My two clients, Du Pont and Unisys, were very supportive.

Jeanette Lerman, the vice president of corporate communications I worked with at Unisys, celebrated my appointment with blinis, borscht, and chicken Kiev at the famous Russian Tea Room on 57th Street. Surrounded by lovely artwork, flowers, and brass samovars, seated at one of the dark red banquettes, she wished me well on my upcoming adventure. After all the dire warnings, I welcomed her support and enthusiasm. She had been to Moscow, and like me, she's a person who collects experiences more than objects.

Alex arranged a weekend seminar on Soviet affairs conducted by university and government officials for all of us who were part of the Soviet project. It was at this meeting that I first met the person who would be my partner for the next two years, Mike Adams. Mike was vice president and associate creative director at Burson-Marsteller in Chicago. I liked him and felt we would make a good team.

One week later, we were off for our first meeting with the Russians in Moscow. Too excited to sleep, I chatted with my seatmate, a Lithuanian on his way home from his first trip to America. A professor at the Institute of Philosophy, Sociology, and Law in Vilnius, he was advocating Lithuanian independence and gave me some pins to wear to support his cause.

As we started to land, I pressed my nose to the window of the Pan Am 747. I felt as if I were a character in an old spy novel—it was gray and rainy, and I couldn't see anything until we were almost on the runway. Although it took us two hours to get our luggage and make our way to the National Hotel, our arrival essentially was uneventful.

As Nick Rudd, one of our team members, and I rode toward downtown Moscow in a big Zil limo that had been arranged for us, we talked about two things: how big everything was—the street and buildings of enormous scale—and how drab and dull. "Nick, you know what it is," I said. "There's no advertising. No billboards, no signs on buses or bus shelters or neon in the windows. No promotion. No brand names."

"Imagine," he said, "the attention one billboard would get when there are no others to compete!"

The National Hotel, facing Red Square, was obviously at one time a grand hotel and is still considered one of Moscow's best, even though it has been poorly maintained over the years. Some sort of mix-up with the reservations resulted in my sharing a room with Mike. I often wondered if this was a test to see whether we could get along together.

That evening we met for dinner with our attorneys from Coudert Brothers, Richard Dean and Mark Vecchio, to plan strategy for next day's meeting with the Russians. Our goal for the week was to keep moving the negotiations forward. What Alex Kroll had signed was simply a letter of intent to work out a joint venture with Vneshtorgreklama (VTR for short), the government-owned international "ad agency."

The original protocol signed by Kroll and Yuri Deomidov, the director general of Vneshtorgreklama, was only a statement of our general intent. The next step was to start shaping a document that would outline in detail what each party would bring to the joint venture.

Our team mapped out the plans for the week. We would introduce ourselves to the Russians at the first meeting by making a presentation of our work and what we would contribute in terms of training in Western marketing and advertising. This training was critical to a society just beginning to convert from strict central government controls on virtually every aspect of the economy to more of a free market system.

One reason we brought Nick Rudd along on this trip was that he was in charge of Y&R's excellent training programs. He had lugged a stack of videotapes and carousel slide trays onto the airplane to illustrate our work.

The next day we went to the offices of the U.S.-U.S.S.R. Trade & Economic Council for our first meeting. We were greeted by a pleasant receptionist, wearing a smile — unusual in a Russian office, I was to learn later. She was young — in her twenties — and wore an attractive skirt and sweater and not much makeup. Her English was excellent, and she directed us cheerfully down a hallway toward a meeting room.

When I walked in, I saw gray industrial carpeting and straight-back chairs. The high, narrow, curtainless windows along one side and harsh fluorescent lighting gave the room an aseptic feeling. Only later, after I'd visited other offices in Moscow, would I realize how nice this freshly painted, bright room was by this city's standards.

Like typical admen anywhere, we started setting up our tapes and slides and videos. Soon after, the Russian delegation led by Deomidov marched in. They lined up on one side of the table and our group sat on the other, making for an extremely formal negotiation setting. At first, everyone seemed uneasy. The Soviets began to relax by smoking cigarettes that reminded me of the strong French Gauloise, and the unventilated room quickly filled with heavy smoke.

Mitch led the meeting for our side. "Let's start with exchanging samples of work," he suggested.

Both sides had agreed to this earlier, but the Soviets said they hadn't brought any work to show. To open the dialogue, they diagrammed their organization on a flip chart and explained how Vneshtorgreklama reported to the U.S.S.R. Chamber of Commerce.

"We'll show you our work now," Mitch offered.

"That's not necessary," Deomidov responded. "We know who you are; we know who Y&R is; you're number one. That's why we signed a protocol with you and not one of the others that wanted to. So that's good enough for us."

It took a moment for Mitch to recover. We had brought along all those tapes and carousels and work and even Nick Rudd to talk about training programs. Nothing is more frustrating to an adman than not being allowed to give his pitch. Each member of our team looked from one to another, silently asking, "What do we do next?"

We ended up spending the morning and even some of the afternoon in a discussion led by Nick on marketing and a hypothetical product introduction. Its benefit was solely to help us get to know each other better. The substance of the discussion was virtually useless, but it did show that we had a lot of training to do. The Soviet system had very little reason for even these executives of the state ad agency to learn marketing communications.

It was an interesting group that sat around that table: Deomidov with dark hair slicked back, his eyes hidden behind darkly tinted glasses. Deomidov's deputy, Leonid Semenov, the classic stocky Russian stereotype—very large, strong features. His total devotion to his country was betrayed by a special affinity: cowboy boots that he discovered while spending time in Oklahoma, his favorite place in the States. Their attorney, Alexander (Sasha) Shpakovsky, a likable young man but one who operated strictly by the book. Roman Diukarev, a junior man with a quick smile who appeared to be there because he spoke English well; and the man we had been led to believe would be their senior representative in our joint venture, Vladimir Tikhonenkov.

As a group, they were pleasant and spoke English surprisingly well. Except for Tikhonenkov, they were shabbily dressed compared to the dark pinstripes and yellow ties of the Americans. I suspected he got a taste of fine clothing and the opportunity to buy from his assignments outside the Soviet Union, in Japan and elsewhere. Our group began referring to him among ourselves as "Vladimir the Slick." The nickname was apropos because he was so polished, and it helped us distinguish him from the many other Vladimirs we were to meet.

We learned a lot about negotiating with the Russians at the dinner we hosted that evening at a cooperative restaurant. These co-op eateries that offered some of the best food in Moscow were among the first private enterprises to open in the Soviet Union. It was a social evening, one that started out with rounds and rounds of toasts with vodka. (What else?) Every toast was a bottoms-up affair with juice-size glasses filled to the top. We toasted us, them, the Americans, the Soviets, Gorbachev, Reagan, Kroll, all the pretty girls in Moscow, all the pretty girls in New York, and more.

I sat across from Semenov at the long bench table. He told me that to toast properly in Russia, I must always hold eye contact with my partner across the table while we both drained our glasses. To do otherwise was bad form.

Our team got back to the hotel well after midnight, and when we spoke about the meeting the next morning, we knew it had been a long evening and would be a longer day. Later, we learned that foreign diplomats in Moscow carry their own glasses with extra thick bottoms to limit the volume of their drinks. We suspected that the Russians may have been drinking mostly water or had false bottoms in their glasses since they seemed much less affected by this party. "A ploy or a test?" I wondered. We never found out for sure.

Most of the discussions that week were dominated by the legal aspects. Both sides were anxious to get moving on the formal document. They wanted to start bringing hard currency into the country. We wanted to validate the press reports in the United States, which rather than emphasizing the preliminary nature of the first protocol, essentially had said that Y&R was in the Soviet Union and gave the impression we were actually open for business.

As the week wore on, jet lag, late nights, and hangovers took their toll. I became somewhat discouraged. "This is going to be a tough assignment," I allowed one evening to Mike. "Can we make it work?" Mike, too, was getting concerned.

I'm not superstitious, but there were some bad omens. For one meeting, Claire Montgomerie (our in-house attorney), Mitch, and I went ahead and were waiting in Vneshtorgreklama's dim little conference room. When no one else showed after a half hour, we found out that Mike, Nick, and Roman were stuck on the tiny elevator that had brought us up the six floors. Those three were large men, and it was a good half hour before a mechanic cranked the elevator to a floor so the doors could be opened. Nick, who can manage almost any situation, stepped out of the elevator drained of color and obviously shaken.

The prospect of getting suitable office space was also not good. At one point in the week, some of us went to look at the space Vneshtorgreklama would provide as part of its contribution to the joint venture. The dark and grimy space—a storefront office now being used by one of its departments, Souvenir Reklama—was on the ground floor of an apartment building across a wide street from the American Embassy.

The man who managed the office apparently didn't want to

move. "It's cold in winter, sometimes so cold that the single-pane glass freezes over. In summer the sun pours in. And there is no air conditioning," he explained.

The subway was not very near, he said, though that wasn't true, and he had a dozen other reasons why we shouldn't accept the space and should demand better. A very excitable man, he spoke no English but he knew some French, and that became our common language. A funny scene: a Soviet and an American negotiating office space in a Moscow snowstorm in shouted bad French.

By the end of the week, we signed another protocol moving the discussions a step forward. But the exhilaration I felt at the beginning of the week was gone. I realized that we wouldn't be in the advertising business, not even in the public relations business, for quite a while. The Soviets needed something even more basic than that—lessons in a market economy based on supply and demand.

For seventy years, the Soviets have lived under a production-oriented command economy that rewards factories for achieving centrally set output goals without regard to profits. This centralized, bureaucratic system provides little incentive for innovation or quality, or for making sure that needed goods are made and distributed where and when they are desired. To make matters worse, goals weren't set with the consuming needs of the people in mind, but with the idea that people need jobs and should be kept working regardless of what their factory produces.

We did see a rudimentary understanding of how to sell product with communications. On our first trip we met with Vitaly Syrokomsky, editor in chief of *Nedelja*, the weekly magazine supplement to *Izvestia*. Syrokomsky, the stereotypical tough-editor type, gruffly barked out questions to us from behind his hand with a cigarette dangling from one side of his mouth. There was no translator, and since Mike's Russian wasn't polished yet and Nick's was only what he remembered from home as a kid, we struggled through the interview. Afterwards, Syrokomsky launched into a discussion about how he considered himself a consumer activist.

"Let me give you an example. I recently helped people get much-desired fruit juice," he boasted.

"Oh, really?" We were interested.

"I got a call from a party higher-up, and he told me there was a lot of inventory of juice, in fact, too much. He wanted my help. So I devised a scheme to get the message out."

"Did you run some ads?" Maybe somebody does have experience here in commercial communications, I began to think.

"Oh, no. Not at all. People wouldn't believe ads. They think they're all propaganda."

"So, what did you do?" Mike struggled recalling his Russian.

"Well, first I got a couple of letters to the editor written about the growing shortage of fruit juice and questioning why there's not more available because it's so important nutritionally. Once those letters ran, I gave assignments to a couple of reporters to survey restaurants and shops and name those that had no fruit juice available.

"Naturally, they began ordering more juice when they saw their names listed, and people started buying more juice. Then I had a couple of doctors write guest columns about the dietary benefits of juice."

"And then what happened?" We were all listening intently.

"Then I got another call from the party higher-up in charge of distribution who told me, 'That's enough; cut it off.' So I stopped the juice stories."

I thought to myself, "Well, I wouldn't call him a consumer advocate. But I guess he knows the power of communications, even if it's serving the party more than the people."

Over the next two months as I made several trips back and forth to continue the negotiations, my energy and emotions seesawed. After the first trip, I questioned whether the amount of money we could make in the foreseeable future was worth the investment required. I wasn't even sure the Vneshtorgreklama people were our best bet for partners.

"They may not have the influence we're going to need," I commented to Mike.

Each time we signed a new protocol, many issues remained open: the value of the Americans, temporary and permanent housing, office space, and multiple-entry visas.

"If Vneshtorgreklama can't pave the way for opening, why do we need them?" I wondered.

"Do we need partners at all?" Mike had his doubts, too.

Kroll pumped us up. It was like a football game. We'd come back from Moscow discouraged and beaten up, and he'd pat us on the back and send us in again. His encouragement and faith in us were both inspirational and motivating, as was the attention coming our way when the news of our jobs spread.

I wrote a farewell memo to the Du Pont account team:

I clearly remember the day Sputnik was launched, the flights of Yuri Gagarin and John Glenn, the Soviet/American link-up and those first steps on the Moon. I wished to be one of those builder/pioneers who explored the new frontiers. Alas, bad eyes and math skills have kept me on Earth. So I launched into advertising. And surely there have been great days of new ideas and soaring spirits.... Now I have the opportunity to be a "cosmonaut" ... well, sort of. Beginning in the new year, I will lead our joint venture in Moscow, Young & Rubicam/Sovero.

Vneshtorgreklama was still dragging its feet. They wouldn't agree to the salary costs of two Westerners, which meant that Y&R would have to pick up the lion's share of my salary and Mike's.

"Send in one person, not two," they suggested.

"No way," Kroll said.

"We want a majority position because Y&R will be providing most of the funding," we demanded.

"No deal," was their response. "We're providing access to you, and we'll transfer people and business from Vneshtorgreklama."

As the legal representatives of the two sides — Claire Montgomerie for Y&R and Sasha Shpakovsky for VTR — hammered out the details, Mike and I spent our time in Moscow working on setting up. The proposed office site near the U.S. Embassy, dark and divided into many tiny cubicles, needed total renovation. We met with Soviet construction people and told them we wanted to knock down all the interior walls, paint everything white, install good-quality industrial carpet, and use a modular open office system shipped in from the West. We asked for plans and estimates.

At the same time, the Soviets tried to sell us on the idea of buying a nineteenth-century mansion that could be purchased only for hard currency and used for both offices and apartments. They wanted something around $1 million; another $1 million would have been required to make the space workable. Whether foreigners could own property in the Soviet Union was still unclear; yet they demanded an answer the day after we inspected the mansion.

"We'll pass," we told them. "We're not ready to make that sort of commitment yet."

As negotiations with Vneshtorgreklama bogged down, I listened to proposals from other potential partners and dealmakers. During one visit, Boris Birshtein showed us offices and apartments we could use immediately in the much-desired Sovincenter — faxes, copiers, telexes, international telephone lines already installed. Sovincenter was the huge complex for international trade fostered by the industrialist Armand Hammer, which included offices, apartments, and a hotel. It was the center of business in the Soviet Union.

Birshtein displayed his clout in Moscow by having the traffic blocked at intersections as his limo carrying us sped through downtown Moscow in the central VIP lane at 60 mph with blue lights flashing.

"What else do you need?" He seemed anxious to please.

"Multiple-entry visas," Mike and I answered in unison.

He picked up the phone and twenty minutes later in walked Alexander Zelenov, deputy chief of protocol of the Ministry of Foreign Economic Relations. Zelenov said he could get our visas in a couple of weeks. (It took our attorneys ten months after they moved to Moscow to get theirs.) But the fulfillment of his promise was conditional upon our signing with Birshtein.

Kroll continued to steer us toward Vneshtorgreklama.

It was an unsettling few months. Even though we hadn't signed a final agreement, two Soviets were assigned as counterparts to Mike and me. Vladimir Vlasov was identified as the senior Soviet because Tikhonenkov decided to work with a marketing consultancy in London. A man named Yuri Pashin was appointed to fill the number-two slot on the Soviet side.

We began to interview to fill other positions. Without real office space, Mike and I parked each day in a corner of the hotel coffeeshop in the lobby of the Sovincenter to meet applicants. It was a funny sight: Mike and me spread out in a corner, working most of the day there, drinking coffee and on a few occasions ordering some food. One after another, clients, construction people, dealdoers paraded in for meetings. No one bothered us. No one seemed to mind that we occupied the space—but it certainly bothered us. We wanted an office.

We first planned to hire three people we would initially call account directors, a financial person to keep the books, a secretary, and a driver/man Friday. It wasn't time for creative people yet.

We knew we couldn't expect much related experience, if any. We wanted them to have some ability with English and some international experience. If they had worked in advertising or sales promotion at all, that would be a real plus. One man who took part in the original negotiations, Roman Diukarev, emerged as the brightest and most aggressive and certainly the best English speaker. He had been trained as a professional interpreter and had served in the Soviet army in Ethiopia as an English-Russian translator. We hired him.

Valery Federov, a favorite of Vlasov's, became another account director, as did Yuriy Pintelin, a quiet man in his late thirties, congenial and eager; and the lean and lanky Mikhail Stroykov.

Fedorov hadn't worked abroad and his English wasn't great, but he was well connected within the Moscow system. His uncle had been deputy minister of oil and gas, and he obviously had grown up among the right class of people in the classless society. He seemed to know everyone in town. If we needed tickets to an event or a meeting with certain people, he picked up the phone and made it happen. We figured we needed someone on the staff with those kinds of connections.

Galina Golantseva, another member of the negotiating team, was the best candidate for the financial director/accountant position. Eventually, we also hired Natalie Belova as a secretary and Volodya as a driver.

On one trip over in early 1989, Mike and I stopped in Finland to enlist the support of Y&R's nearest office, both for creative back-up and logistics. While there, we looked into ordering audiovisual equipment and selected two office cars at the local Ford dealer, Y&R's biggest client. We ordered a Scorpio sedan and a Sierra station wagon, both with four-wheel drive for tough Moscow winters.

Here it was several months after our first meeting with the Russians. We had a staff; we were ready to start renovation; we had made arrangements to order furniture, cars, and equipment; we even had a few client nibbles. But we had no joint venture agreement.

We decided to proceed anyway and even held our first staff meeting in a rented conference room in the Sovincenter. The room was set up with a U-shaped table.

"Here, sit at the head of the table with me," I suggested to Vlasov.

"No, that's your place. You're the boss. I'll sit here." He pointed to the chair on my right, which was on a leg of the U.

It was the first time that I realized Vlasov intended to defer to me about business matters. He knew that we were doing a fifty-fifty deal, but with this gesture he implied that he recognized Mike and I would provide the know-how. I appreciated the pride he must have had to sacrifice. The staff seemed to understand its significance also. Around the table were the people who would determine the future of this agency for the next few years. They were solemn, yet eager to learn. They too were taking a risk by betting that their country was moving toward capitalism and a better future.

The meeting only lasted about ninety minutes, but it set the tone for my tenure. "We will have regular training sessions; we will handle clients Western style; we will adopt the Y&R philosophy of being problem solvers, not mechanics." I wanted to be quite clear about this.

I laid out how I expected the office would operate. "First and foremost, our focus will be on clients. As a service business, we will have to work nights and weekends when necessary. That is the way Y&R became a leading international agency. That is the way to be successful. We will base our recommendations to clients on sound research. We will price our services fairly and pay the media fairly."

It wasn't atypical in the Soviet Union for organizations to overcharge customers and underpay suppliers. "This is not the way we will operate. We will be fair," I emphasized again.

"We are not in this for the short term — we want to establish ourselves as a reputable and leading company in this business for the long haul."

I told them, "Training sessions will be every Saturday morning from nine to twelve."

"Not possible," Vlasov spoke up, and others echoed his objection. They refused to miss the weekends at their dachas in the countryside and the precious Saturday-morning time for shopping. We settled on Tuesday and Thursday from 7:30 to 9:00 A.M. before the office opened.

Officially, this first meeting in January was no big deal. Yet to me it was a watershed. We had what appeared to be a good staff, who wanted to learn and work. We had set some goals. I thought, "This might be the most rewarding job I'll ever have, after all."

But by then, Kroll was losing patience with the protracted negotiations and essentially said, "Next time, don't come back without a deal." That sort of took the teeth out of any negotiating power we had. The signing itself was a nonevent. At 5:00 P.M. Moscow time on January 26, 1989, Deomidov and I initialed each page and signed the deal.

When Y&R/Sovero — the name that eventually evolved from Y&R/Vneshtorgreklama or Y&R/VTR — officially was born, we

already had an assignment from a Spanish marketer of processed meats and were doing several market studies, including
research for Johnson & Johnson sanitary protection products.

I sent Kroll a corny telex saying something like THE EAGLE
HAS LANDED. It was anticlimactic, but I did feel that a great
adventure was finally really under way.

We called all the suppliers we had placed orders with and
told them to go ahead and execute—get us the furniture,
audiovisual equipment, phones, faxes, telex, photocopiers,
cars, and so on, all the stuff we couldn't get in the Soviet
Union and had to ship in. We could operate like an agency
even from a rented conference room for now, but by March
we should be in our new offices. Or so I thought.

Mike and I were still struggling with the living accommodations problem. The Soviets continued to say, "Trust us. The
apartments will be here for you when you're ready. Don't
worry. We're working on it." Neither Mike nor I planned to
have our families come over before the end of the summer, so
we figured it was something we'd just put up with.

Up to this point, Mike and I had traveled together. We
decided that as we were now officially open, we should start
alternating our stays so that at least one of us was in the
"office" at all times.

The staff would continue to work out of their current office
space for the time being—most were Vneshtorgreklama
employees. Some would work on research projects; others
would try to take care of all the details to get our new office
into order—make sure everything was moving along, the
construction, equipment, registration, multiple-entry visas
for Mike and me and our families. Our staff would get good
hands-on experience in how to start up an office, Western
style. I hoped that I had the grace, patience, and good humor
that this job inevitably would demand.

2

THE OFFICIAL OPENING

MIKE AND I WALKED BRISKLY TOWARD 11A DRUZHINNIKOVSKAYA Street. The wind whipped about the fresh fallen snow and the sidewalks, although cleared, were icy. It was still winter here in the Soviet capital, even though April was almost over. As we turned the corner onto Druzhinnikovskaya, we stopped for a moment to take a look at the broad boulevard lined with sticks for trees and no hint yet of a leaf sprout. Mike especially was pleased with the location, not far from the U.S. Embassy, and on a beautiful expanse with a nice park across the way.

We were making this trip together to the construction site to try to speed along the renovation at 11A. Just that morning, I'd had a call from Ellen Goldman, the young New York interior designer we were working with to furnish the office. She understood exactly what we needed — something flexible that would grow with what we expected to be a rapidly changing agency. We also were installing a shower and some furniture that could serve as cots at night in case Mike and I didn't get apartments soon. The Westinghouse prefabricated modular office furniture Ellen had recommended, and the resilient carpeting made of Du Pont's Antron fiber, were ready and waiting to be shipped from the States. (Happily, both Westinghouse and Du Pont were Y&R clients.)

Conscientiously, she was calling to find out whether we had a shipping date for her yet.

"Regretfully, no," I told her. "The office still looks like a war zone."

It was more than a month after we had planned to be in our office. The glass and wood partitions that had divided the space into tiny cubicles had been torn down, and the dark cabinetry and fake walnut paneling had been ripped out, but the inside was littered with old two-by-fours and chunks of plaster. Outside was a huge pile of debris, ready to be carted away.

Vlasov had been unable to speed up progress on the renovation, so Mike and I made the trek down. Mike, who knows Russian, spoke with the workers. No, they didn't know anything about the work being completed a month ago. He should talk to the boss.

"Where is he?"

"He should be here some time today. But we never know exactly when he'll show up."

"How can we get this moving faster?" Mike asked them.

They just shrugged. Eventually, he pulled one of them aside. "Probably another month and a half before the space will be usable," Mike interpreted.

"That's unacceptable," I fumed.

Mike was as unhappy as I was working in hotel lobbies and coffeeshops. The staff were getting restless in their old offices, and I suspected they would be much more productive in our own space. I had strong suspicions that they were being required to work on Vneshtorgreklama business while Y&R/Sovero was paying their full salaries. We had already lost three staffers—Mikhail Stroykov, Yuriy Pintelin, and Galina Golantseva—perhaps avoidable if we had had our own adequate working quarters and conditions. Natalie was threatening to leave because she couldn't work with Vlasov, either.

As Mike and I walked back to our hotel, we talked about what kind of celebration we should plan for the official opening. We wanted to do something special.

A few days later we flew back to the States. "Just six more weeks of this commuting back and forth," I thought. "What a relief."

Back in New York, I prepared to entertain Vlasov and Pashin, who were on their first trip to America for Y&R/Sovero. I sat in my New York office waiting for the phone to ring. They would fly to Chicago first, where Mike would take care of them for a few days as they attended a Y&R-sponsored management conference at Northwestern University's Kellogg School. Then they would come to New York.

I couldn't wait to hear from Mike about their reaction to Chicago. I was engrossed in working out office assignments when his call came. "We're not getting the office space on Druzhinnikovskaya Street" were the first words I heard him say. Vlasov had brought the news.

I was shocked and angry. "After all these months. No way. That's *totally* unacceptable."

"It doesn't look good, Gary." Mike was upset but realistic.

Vlasov was not willing to give any kind of explanation, Mike told me. Just, "It's not going to work." Vlasov repeatedly gave Mike the same answer.

Later, Mike pulled Pashin aside. "Trust me," Pashin said. "Don't fight for this one." Eventually, Mike got fed up and demanded an explanation from Pashin.

"Somebody's objected to our being there," Pashin said.

"Damn it, who's 'somebody'?" Mike had no more patience. "VTR owns that space. You should be able to do what you want with it in the joint venture."

Finally, everything made sense to Mike. "Gary, that 'somebody' must be our favorite law enforcement organization. Pashin never actually came right out and confirmed it, but he never denied it, either."

"So why do you think so?" I asked him.

"You know, there seems to be some special activity being conducted from the top floor of that building we're in."

The office was situated perfectly for surveillance of the U.S. Embassy directly across the way, and on the top floor of our building they could be beaming various pieces of sophisticated listening equipment at "the enemy." Our convenient location was convenient for the Soviets, too. I tried to remember if I'd seen or heard anything suspicious, but nothing came to mind.

"Those guys probably aren't really comfortable with a joint venture ad agency on the first floor, especially with Americans in it."

Furious, I picked up the phone to call John Cooper, head of legal services at Y&R. He was just as furious.

"What are we going to do, John? I can't keep working in hotel lobbies."

"We'll work it out," he said, trying to calm me down despite his own concern.

Vyacheslav Malkevich, head of the Chamber of Commerce, was coming to the States within the next few weeks, so we devised a plan to invite him to a nice dinner in Washington, D.C., that Alex Kroll would host. At that meeting we planned to put the issue of office space on the table.

"He must understand our position on this," John said.

"He's got to understand that the jv is in jeopardy."

The dinner was held at a fancy hotel in suburban Washington. Malkevich and Golanov, his number-two man, were both there. John artfully maneuvered the conversation so that there could be no doubt in their minds that we felt they weren't living up to their bargain to provide office space.

Malkevich, whose department could be likened to the U.S. Department of Commerce, would have been embarrassed to concede he couldn't deliver. He's an important and powerful man, and hates to admit there's anything he can't do within his country.

Once back in Moscow, he did take action within the boundaries of his authority. He moved out the Marine Arbitration Commission reporting to him in the Sovincenter to the space on Druzhinnikovskaya Street and gave us their space in the Sovincenter.

Knowing why we were banned from Druzhinnikovskaya Street, we suspected even Malkevich wouldn't win a fight for that space.

As an "apology" and goodwill gesture for the additional six months' delay it would take to get this space ready, he arranged for Mike and me finally to get apartments. We figured that the Soviets were so embarrassed at what had happened with the first office space that someone powerful stepped in and made sure we got what we needed. "You'll have apartments at the Sovincenter also," Vlasov said happily when we got back to Moscow.

Although frustrated that we had to go through all the renovation aggravation from scratch again, I was delighted to have the apartment situation resolved. At least we wouldn't have to live in the office. We still had to finish converting 11A into workable space because Y&R/Sovero was displacing the Chamber's Marine Arbitration Commission in the Sovincenter, and that department was moving into 11A Druzhinnikovskaya.

Mike, Vlasov, and I took a look at our new office space. It was slightly larger than 11A, but also divided into tiny rabbit-warren spaces. The walls were papered with the typical dark flocked wallpaper, and an industrial yellow linoleum covered the floors. Well above the street on the thirteenth floor, windows spanned one wall, and we could see the Moscow River and Moscow State University in the distance, a nice tree-lined park not so far away. Not bad.

"We'll have to redecorate," I said.

"No need," Vlasov objected. "It's fine. No need to spend good hard money." As usual, Vlasov was already on the way to the bank with "his" hard currency.

"We have the modular furniture. We've already paid for it. It was custom-designed. And we're not working in this kind of atmosphere."

"You shouldn't have ordered it without consulting me. Send it back."

"Vladimir, you approved the specs."

Grudgingly, he admitted that was true.

We pushed the construction crew to get 11A finished, and within a few weeks our new space was vacated. This time Vlasov proved his worth by hiring a demolition crew that came in at night (moonlighters, actually) and in one week pulled out all the partitions, tore down the wallpaper, ripped up layers of linoleum. Within another couple of days, the new work could start.

The department that moved out left two functioning telephones, so as soon as the demolition crew finished, Mike and I started working in the new space even as the renovation was going on around us. We sat at a card table with two folding chairs. I wrote "Y&R/Sovero" on a Post-It note and stuck it on the door. We were in business.

That was when we were "discovered" by the producer for the Ted Koppel show, Tara Sonnenschein, who was about to start taping the TV special called *Revolution in a Box*. There in the midst of our empty office space, seated around a card table, Mike and I were interviewed on camera about the impact of commercial television in the Soviet Union.

The walls were in such poor condition that they had to be covered with wallpaper to hide the cracks. That done, everything was painted white, and our carpeting was put in. But since this space was larger than the first, there wasn't enough of the already cut gray carpeting. Ellen devised a scheme for using a purple border around the whole office that picked up the color of one of the flecks in the main piece of carpeting. It looked as if it were planned that way. She was ingenious in reconfiguring the 11A furnishings and equipment we already had, and ended up making use of about 90 percent of the furniture.

I got the apartment at about the same time: a small one-bedroom, but certainly convenient to the office, just across the building lobby from one tower to the next. The Soviets tried so hard to fix it up and make it extra nice for me with fresh wallpaper, beige and brown wheat stalks—Soviet chic. They installed new dark brown industrial carpeting, which matched the brown sofa, brown armchairs, and brown seat covers on the dining-room chairs. I really appreciated the intent, but I knew Freddye would want to redo it in a way that both of us would find more palatable.

"It's so nice to be able to leave a few things in Moscow rather than have to pack up everything each time I come back to the States," I told Freddye my next trip home.

I could also walk to work—down one elevator bank, across the lobby, and up another row of elevators. My commute took five minutes, compared to the hour and fifteen minutes I traveled in New York. I finally began to feel that we would actually get a business started.

My next goal was to have the office look like a Y&R office by the time of the first board meeting. That was in mid-October, three months away. Virtually everything was on order. It was just a matter of getting the furniture and equipment delivered and installed. By now, though, I knew that the seemingly simplest of tasks could hit major snags.

The weeks flew by. Surprisingly, the office cars arrived from Helsinki without a hitch. The furniture got hung up in England where it had been shipped first from the United States so that European-style electrical work could be done. Then it got hung up somewhere at the port of entry in the Soviet Union.

Ellen was on standby to come to Moscow as soon as the furniture arrived so that she could make sure it was installed properly. We finally got a delivery date and the time was set. On the third weekend in September, Ellen flew in. Two British technicians from Westinghouse, the furniture manufacturer, came with their wrenches to do the installation. Panels, some covered with white or wood grain laminate, some with blue fabric, were transformed into desks and cabinets and office dividers, all within twenty-eight hours. The crew worked almost round the clock, sleeping in the office space because they felt it was better than their hotel.

The biggest obstacle was the conference room table. As the Russians unloaded the 12-foot table from the delivery truck and tried to get it into the elevator, they shook their heads.

"Won't fit," they grunted, and started to put it back in the truck.

"That's simple. You just take the top of the elevator cab off and stand the table on end," Ellen suggested. She had seen that done numerous times in New York City. Alas, Russian workmen had never done such a thing before, so naturally it couldn't be done.

Mike and Ellen huddled. "Do you think we can get some-one to carry it up to the thirteenth floor using the service stairs?" We weren't sure. Volodya volunteered to try and find some husky laborers. It wasn't long before he was back.

"A bottle of booze and a carton of cigarettes for each of the guys will do it," he said. They carried the table up the twelve flights. They dropped it once and damaged a corner, but at that point we were just happy to have our conference table in place.

The chairs were in another shipment, but Volodya some-how managed to scrounge up enough for the staff and brought them in one by one as Mike, Ellen, and I were clean-ing up late Sunday night. When Volodya walked in, his eyes bugged out. I couldn't imagine why he looked so shocked, and asked Mike. (Despite lessons, my Russian skills were still virtually nonexistent.)

Apparently the sight of the CEO of a company vacuuming the carpet, putting together furniture, and doing other menial work on his hands and knees was more than he could believe.

It was important to have the office look its best the next Monday morning when the staff saw it put together for the first time. Freddye went out and bought champagne and flowers for the occasion. As the staff walked in, many of them had tears in their eyes. They now had concrete evidence that all their hard work was paying off.

"You were right to do it this way, Gary." Even Vlasov was moved.

Giddy, they walked from one space to another, flipped light switches on and off, opened and closed the smooth-gliding drawers in their desks, fingered the pens, pencils, and paperclips they saw generously spread around. It was a magical moment as we had our first staff meeting in our own conference room.

"You should be very proud of what you've accomplished," I told them. "This is a taste of the special rewards your hard work will bring. This system can be beat. But we've still got work to do. The board meeting is just a month away. We still need to get in our a/v equipment, telex, phones, fax, and copier. So let's get down to business."

It was understandable that they weren't very productive that day, but they made up for it in the month that followed. I called Helsinki, where we already had selected audiovisual equipment, and told them to ship. Vlasov and I went to Siemens to follow up our order for the fax and telex equipment and phone system.

One of the first things I realized was that I had to teach the staff how to answer the phone. Typically, when you call an office in Moscow, you hear a brusque *"Slushayu"* (literally, "I'm listening") in a low, gruff voice.

"We want callers to know what company they've reached," I explained. "It's the first impression we make. So we'll answer, 'Y&R/Sovero,' in a pleasant tone." By the end of the first week, most had caught on—the youngest first, the older staffers eventually.

Vlasov made some demands of his own. "If we're going to operate Western style, we need a safe," he told me when we began ordering our equipment.

"What do we need a safe for?" I asked. "We're not going to have anything that valuable."

"Oh, yes. We've got to have somewhere to keep the money and the documents."

"What documents? We don't have any secrets. We can keep a copy of the jv documents in a locked file. The building is locked; the office is locked. There are guards everywhere. We have an alarm system. What's the safe for?"

"No, no. Every Soviet office must have a safe. It's required." He was adamant.

"All right, we'll order a small one and put it on a bookshelf."

"No, that won't do. It's got to be substantial."

I didn't want to fight with him any more, so I gave him a catalogue and asked him to select the one that he thought was appropriate. He picked a cast-iron safe—about 4 by 4 feet—weighing at least 1,000 pounds.

We needed a forklift to move it around and I can't imagine how many cartons of cigarettes it must have cost to get it up to the thirteenth floor. We put it at one end of the office.

"Okay, Vladimir, you have your safe. What are you going to put in it?"

"Well, we have the petty cash."

That was about 50 rubles—either $85 or $5 depending on what conversion rate you used, official or black market. We kept the employee records in there, and Mike and I started keeping our ruble salaries in it.

Then one day some official came to inspect and told us it was illegal to keep more than 100 rubles in petty cash. The most valuable things we kept in it were makeup kits we used for favors.

There were other unexpected surprises for me. When the supplies arrived from New York and everyone could proudly display their own stapler and roll of Scotch tape on their desks, they were like kids on the first day of school with a brand-new box of Crayola crayons. For the staff, these supplies were definitely signs of prestige.

The accountant—one of Yuri's several predecessors—was fascinated by the Casio adding machine that worked on batteries. He'd never seen an AA battery before. But as he searched through his desk and file drawers, I noticed that he was growing quite agitated.

"What's the problem, Valery?" I couldn't imagine what was troubling him.

"There's no carbon paper here." He looked fearful.

Most bookkeeping in the Soviet Union is still done the old-fashioned way, by hand in huge ledgers. The carbon paper was needed to produce the duplicates we required.

"Just go out and buy some, Valery," I said, to calm him down.

"Gary, there's none in Moscow. I've already searched."

"Here, take some hard currency and go to the Mezh stationery store." I went to Vlasov's huge safe to take out money for him.

He came back in less than an hour even more distraught. "They don't have any, either. I won't be able to do my job properly."

Once again, I told him not to worry, that we would find some. I called Y&R in Stockholm. "Remember you said if I needed anything I could rely on you," I reminded my friend and colleague, Brian Harrison, who ran that office.

Carbon paper was practically obsolete in Sweden, he told me. "We haven't used it for years." I explained how important the paper was and asked that he try to find some. He must have found a box that had been on the back shelf of a Swedish office supply store for years, because it was dusty and somewhat worn around the edges when it arrived by air express the next day. To Valery, it was heaven-sent.

The equipment began arriving piecemeal. We got the audiovisual equipment but no cables for the VCR. The lens for the slide projector was missing. The chairs came but no hexkey to assemble them.

Every morning I scheduled a staff meeting in the conference room to discuss priorities, and the entire staff got caught up in the spirit of meeting our deadlines. It was a good lesson for them to understand that each day they were expected to give a progress report. Their assignments, whether directly related to a client project or setting up the office, would not go away. Each day they must give a status report.

The first time we held a morning meeting, it lasted well over an hour. Much as I tried to get the meeting moving, the Soviets sipped their coffee and gossiped in between important business, enjoying the ambience of their new conference room. So, after that, I set a rule that we would hold the morning meetings standing up unless it was a training session or special long-term discussion.

"You can bring in your coffee and your notepads, but no sitting," I told them.

We'd go around the room and staffers, one by one, would discuss the work planned for the day — what needed to be accomplished and how they were going about it. During this time, we assigned the use and priority of the cars. Volodya drove the fancier European Ford Scorpio, used primarily for clients and meetings. The workhouse Ford Sierra station wagon hauled equipment and supplies into the office. Under our "standing policy," we were able to cut down meeting time to about a half hour.

The date that the photocopier was to arrive came and went with no notification of delivery. After another day passed, I got nervous and called Xerox in London. I asked to speak to the regional vice president whom I had met when he was traveling through Moscow a couple of months earlier. Xerox is a client of Y&R's in many parts of the world.

"I'm calling you as a client, not as your ad agency," I said. "We're really depending on you to have the copier here so we can get to work."

"I'm terribly sorry. Let me get right on it."

The next day I received a fax saying that instead of shipping the copier overland, Xerox was air-freighting it in at their expense, a gesture of support and customer service that we greatly appreciated.

Volodya went to the cargo area at the airport to pick it up. He came back with a stack of papers.

"Bad news. Bad news," he kept saying over and over.

"What's the matter, Volodya?"

"You see these papers. We have to get twenty-five signatures here to pick up the copier, and they're all from the militia. That office is open only about two hours a week. We'll never get this done in time."

We learned for the first time that installing a copier required permission from the militia because of government sensitivity to any kind of equipment that produced copies. Soviet laws required that the copier be installed in a locked room approved by the militia or that a guard be hired to watch over its use. This, I was told, was because a copier could be used to reproduce subversive materials.

"We're not operating under those conditions," I told Volodya. "No way are we going to let this hold up our opening. Please go over to the Chamber of Commerce protocol office and ask them to help us."

"Ah, I never thought of that," he admitted. Two days later, the copier was delivered and installed—right out in plain view in our reception area. I'm not sure how he did it, whether he pulled strings himself or whether the Chamber helped. Maybe he simply "kidnapped" our copier from the airport.

Just as the phone and fax equipment were to arrive, the Moscow airport refused to accept any more foreign deliveries. They were so overloaded with goods being shipped in for an upcoming American trade fair, they couldn't handle any more shipments. But I wasn't going to allow that to get in our way, either.

I asked Mike to take a one-day turnaround trip to Düsseldorf to pick up the equipment and carry it in as personal luggage. Bit by bit, everything was finally falling into place.

When the week of the board meeting arrived, October 9, 1989, I was nervous but proud of my staff and their accomplishments. All the loose ends weren't neatly tied up, but the most important, obvious ones were. The phones weren't all workable yet, but they were connected at everyone's desk. The chairs finally came and were assembled the night before. The best part was that the office didn't look much different than if it were a Y&R office in any other country. It wasn't fancy, but neat, clean, and efficient.

As I chatted with Alex Kroll and his wife Phyllis in the car on the way back from the airport, I thought about my conversation with him a year earlier. I hadn't expected setting up the office to take this long. Looking back now, I felt we had accomplished it in record time by Soviet standards. We basked in compliments from our visitors, although I'm sure they didn't fully appreciate what we had achieved.

The board meeting proceeded as expected. Vlasov presented a report on the market situation. I followed that with our business plan. Seith Rothstein, our financial and business affairs manager out of New York, and Yuri Birasov, our accountant, reviewed the financials. It was routine for many of the board members; for me, Mike, and the staff, it was a major milestone.

3

BEATING THE SYSTEM

I LOOKED AT MY WATCH. IT WAS 4:00 A.M. I WAS WIDE AWAKE. THIS was getting to be a bad habit.

As our official opening day—set for October 14, 1989—came closer, I was waking up every day at this time. I looked around the room: it was still dark, but despite being small, the place felt light and airy. Freddye's attempt to make us forget where we were with modern Swedish furniture had worked. Here and throughout the three-room apartment, she had covered the dark brown wall-to-wall carpeting with pale beige throw rugs, and selected occasional tables and cabinets with plenty of glass and clean, simple lines. I left the dark heavy burden of Moscow behind me each time I walked through the front door.

Restless, I climbed out of bed, but not before the list of to-do's started racing through my mind—over and over. There were so many things to get done before we opened in October. And that was just a month away.

We still had to get the copier, the phones, furniture, the conference-room table, audiovisual equipment, the computers, and on and on. But at the top of my list was the telex line. That telex number was becoming an obsession with me.

It had been on Vlasov's "to-do" list for months.

"If Vlasov doesn't get the telex number on Monday, there's going to be hell to pay," I'd told Mike last week.

As I took a shower and got ready for work, my emotions seesawed between the thrill of the official opening and fear that we would not be ready when Y&R senior management got here. Alex Kroll, the chairman, would be coming, along with Jim Dowling, the CEO of Y&R's public relations subsidiary, Burson-Marsteller. This would be their first visit to the new office, and I wanted it to look like any real Y&R office. I wanted Alex to be proud of "his baby."

Alex's expectations were high, and no one, especially me, wanted to disappoint him. When Alex told me I was to be Y&R's man in Moscow, he had placed his trust in me to fulfill a dream for him, and I wanted him to know that trust was well placed.

Opening the first Western ad agency in the Soviet Union was a way he could put his stamp on Y&R. I certainly didn't want to be the one to spoil that vision.

By the time I was ready to make the short trip down the elevator in my apartment building, across the lobby, and up another elevator bank to the office, I had worked myself up over the telex again. I stormed into the conference room where the staff were waiting for me to start our regular nine o'clock staff meeting. This was a stand-up meeting I had instituted early on to ensure that we all understood the day's assignments and priorities.

After a quick "Good morning" and halfhearted pleasantries, I got straight to the point. "Vlasov, the status of the telex. Where the hell is it?"

"Difficult, very difficult," he muttered, staring down at his shoes.

I was abrupt. "I've heard 'Difficult, very difficult,' too many times. This is one of your responsibilities and I expect it done immediately. No more delays. No more excuses. We *must* be able to communicate."

The staff stood with their mouths agape. I hadn't pushed Vlasov for the telex line until several weeks ago because we only recently moved into the office and even more recently received the equipment from Siemens. So it wasn't especially high priority until now.

Now the brand-new telex equipment—which I unpacked and put together myself—had been sitting idle for more than a week. Months before I had picked the number we would apply for. I had spent some time mulling over what we should choose. YRSOVERO was too long. So I settled on ADPR, short for ADvertising and Public Relations.

I was like a madman. But that telex was to be our life line. Telephones were unreliable, so faxes were unreliable. Even though I had been here almost a year, I still felt isolated when I couldn't get an international phone line. From the time I first arrived in Moscow in September 1988, through my days of commuting in the winter, spring, and summer of 1989, until Freddye finally joined me that fall, I never liked being so out of touch. Even after Freddye arrived, we worried that our daughters or parents might not able to reach us when they needed to. Happily, there were no real business or personal emergencies, but I was always concerned that there would be a time when we had to make a call and couldn't. I wanted a reliable method of communication and the telex was it.

"Vlasov, this is something *you* have to do. I can't get it done. This is your system, your people. Please get it done."

I got the same unsatisfactory response. "We'll get it done."

"Now!" I was adamant.

Once again, he sent off two of the staff, Volodya, our driver/man Friday, and Fedorov, our "connected" one, with the proper papers and application to get the number. Once again, they came back after several hours with their heads hanging and defeat on their faces.

I just bitched louder.

The next day, Vlasov told Pashin to go with them. "Maybe as the number-two Soviet in our office, he can throw his weight around," Vlasov told me.

That was sort of ironic. Yuri Pashin was as atypical of the tough-talking Soviet stereotype as you could get. Mild-mannered and eager to please, Pashin reminded me of a friendly insurance salesman. With his wonderfully ready smile, he'd be more likely to charm someone into issuing the number than to use clout. But charm apparently didn't work, either.

He, too, came back defeated.

"I'm going myself, Vlasov," I said.

"No, no, you can't do that." He looked worried.

"What's the problem?"

"No, you can't go. The woman that issues the numbers doesn't speak English," he explained. I began to understand the power of this one woman whose signature was required to authorize the issuance of all telex numbers. When she is sick or out or uncooperative, nothing happens ... in the whole Soviet Union.

"Well, one of the staff can go with me and translate." The language barrier had never stopped me from getting out of the office before.

"No, the office is in a building where foreigners are not allowed."

I was no stranger to not being allowed into certain buildings. On one of my first trips to Moscow to meet with Vnesh-torgreklama people in their own offices, a guard stepped in front of me and spat, *"Nyet!"*, blocking me from entering the building. It took some persuasion from one of the Soviets with me before the guard stepped aside and let me pass.

I wasn't convinced, however, that being barred from the telex building was the real reason for the stonewalling.

Finally, Vlasov opened up a bit. He admitted that the big obstacle was the woman herself. Her signature was required as part of the authorization process to get a telex line issued, and her reputation as the wicked witch of Moscow was widespread. For no apparent reason, she'd simply turn down and delay applications. She had been giving them a tough time all along. Whether Vlasov himself had gone and been so intimidated by her that he never went back himself, I don't know. All I knew was he'd been sending some of the staff periodically. He apparently was quite embarrassed that at his level he couldn't get assigned a telex number from someone who was essentially a clerk.

"All right," I told Pashin and Fedorov. By now I had no patience to go through the proper chain of command and tell Vlasov how I wanted this handled. I gave explicit instructions directly to the two men.

"You guys go back one more time, and this is what you are to say and all you are to say: *'What do you want?'*"

They left, somewhat puzzled at my instructions. Within a short time they were back, grinning. "She says she wants a blue sweater with these little pearls sewn across the neck and it should be a size fourteen."

"Is this for her?" I asked incredulously.

"No, it's for her daughter." They were still grinning. Apparently, she had already outfitted herself and was now working on dressing her whole family.

I was amazed at the details they related. "How does she know exactly what she wants?"

"She saw it in a *beriozka* shop," they told me. "And," I thought to myself, "obviously was just waiting for the right opportunity to spring the request."

"Done." I told them to take some hard currency, go to the *beriozka* shop, and buy the $40 sweater. *Beriozka* shops started out as the foreign currency shops open only to foreigners, but later became available to privileged Soviets with hard currency.

That wasn't the only time we had to use additional incentives to get work done in this "workers' paradise." We wanted nice rooms at the Mezh Hotel when Kroll and Dowling came in for the first board meeting. Since our partner here was the Chamber of Commerce and since the Chamber also ran the Mezh, we figured we wouldn't have any problem getting rooms, especially since we knew the dates and had reserved two months in advance.

A week before they were to arrive, I asked Natalie, our secretary, to check to make sure we were all set and found out that no rooms were available.

"Not acceptable," I told her. "We have to have those rooms. Go back and tell them we made those reservations two months ago."

Two days went by and we still couldn't get the Mezh to promise us rooms. Late one afternoon, Natalie slipped into my office. "Gary," she said, "if you want to make sure we get those rooms, you need to buy two cartons of cigarettes and two makeup kits down in the *beriozka* shop."

"Ah." Things were beginning to make sense.

While we were at it, we bought a dozen makeup kits. They weren't that expensive; maybe $18 each. And every time we needed rooms at the Mezh for visitors, we knew exactly how to reserve them. To the ladies behind the desk, who had no access to nice cosmetics, the kits were solid gold.

In a society where only the privileged with hard currency could participate in a separate cash economy, those without resorted to other methods to obtain a few luxuries. Many refused to perform their assigned tasks without something special in return. It certainly rankled my midwestern sense of values and standards to participate in this "barter" economy.

Makeup kits and cigarettes weren't the only "new methods" of doing business that I had to learn. Patience was another.

Joe DeDeo, a senior executive of Y&R in London, and a friend and counselor throughout my career, had warned, "Moscow might not be the right place for you."

I was demanding of myself and my staff. I pushed people, and I expected results. Patience was not one of my outstanding virtues. People who have worked in the Soviet Union and other parts of Eastern Europe say that after your toothbrush, the next thing you better have with you is patience.

Joe had advised against my going to Moscow, but for the first time in my career I acted against his advice. There were many times when his words of warning came back to haunt me.

My management style didn't include "It can't be done." If you're blocked in accomplishing a task, then you figure out another way. And if you're blocked again, you come up with still another solution. That was not an easy lesson for the Soviets to learn. The Soviet system is rigid. Resignation is a common trait; you see very little feistiness, creativity, and drive among the Soviets because their system has for years beaten them down. Innovation and initiative are discouraged in a totalitarian system. Besides, there's not much incentive or reward for doing an extra special job. Most Soviets get paid the same regardless of their proficiency, and it's quite rare that anyone is ever fired. Attendance means as much as accomplishment.

As the American partners, Mike and I had an obligation to our Soviet partners to teach them how business is conducted in the West. In some ways, it was like recalling some of those old sayings that your parents tried to instill in you as a child. "If at first you don't succeed, try, try again."

These were quite intelligent people, and I didn't want to insult them, but I had to find a way to teach them certain basics that Americans learned as children at the same time as more advanced business techniques. Certainly, it was challenging.

Regardless of the exact specifications of the formal agreement, we personally felt a responsibility to show them our way of doing business, how to set goals and achieve them.

Sometimes the staff would shake their heads when I was ranting and raving. They had never seen anyone like Mike and me who wouldn't take no for an answer. For our Soviet staff, each week was another chapter in "The Y&R Guys Against the System."

Accustomed to standing in line for hours or days and facing frequent rejection, the Soviets easily accepted that a simple assignment could take weeks. *Izvestia,* the Soviet newspaper, reported in 1985 that Soviet consumers spent 65 billion hours each year standing in line. The average housewife was reported to spend three hours a day shopping — for necessities, not luxuries.

Our staffers would often start an explanation of why they hadn't accomplished an assignment with "State regulations require that ..."

"Stop," I would interrupt. "This is *our* venture. This is the job *we* have to get done. We'll do it the way *we* want to."

They would smile at me smugly and say nothing, but the

message on their faces was: "He'll learn. Just give him time."

I never gave in without a fight. Not too long after Freddye and I moved into the apartment, I casually dropped some mail in a box as I was on my way to the office across the lobby of the Mezh. My mind was preoccupied with all the issues at hand. Just as I released the letters, I realized that the post office box was another ten feet away and that I had dropped the mail into the Sovincenter suggestion box, which looked much the same.

"Damn." I was annoyed at first. Then as I thought about the idea of a suggestion box in the Mezh, I was amused. The whole society was so anti-service that a suggestion box was curious indeed.

I went to the nearby office and managed to get the attention of a clerk.

"Excuse me," I said. "I've made a mistake. I've put my mail in the suggestion box." I pointed to it.

"No, that's not the mailbox," she said, turning back to her work. She was a typical Russian hotel clerk, not wanting to be bothered. "That's down there," she pointed to the postal box.

"Yes, I realize that now. But I made a mistake. It's sort of the same shape and size. If we can just get the key…"

"Oh, no," she interrupted me. "That's not possible. That's too bad."

"Look, there's just a tiny little lock on the top. Maybe somebody knows where the key is."

She asked around, and no one knew anything about a key. Most didn't even know a suggestion box existed.

"I'll have to call the manager." It sounded like a threat.

"Terrific. Then I can take out my letters and put them in the right slot."

The manager came down from the executive offices. He

was as puzzled as the clerks. "No, we've never had a key to that box," he said.

"You mean you've never opened the box in ten years?" I wasn't really surprised.

"No, we've never done that."

"Well, just give me a claw hammer and I'll have that lock off in two seconds."

"Oh, no, Mr. Burandt, we couldn't do that."

"Well, how are you going to get the suggestions out? Much less my mail?"

"I don't know. We'll have to go to a higher authority. You'll have to wait."

The manager went away and eventually came back after another search of offices. I could tell nothing was going to happen right away, and after investing an hour on personal mail that I didn't think was that important, I decided to leave.

"We'll let you know," he promised.

He never notified me, but the letters finally found their way to the recipients, so someone must have opened the suggestion box and transferred the letters to the mailbox. I suspect there was other mail that could have been there for years because I'm sure other people must have made the same mistake.

Getting the agency name on the directory in the lobby of our office building was another long-drawn-out hassle. Week after week, I asked Vlasov, "Why isn't our name up? We need to let people know we're here."

"Things take time here. I'm working on it."

Having our name on the directory was important because we expected walk-in business. When people saw Y&R on the directory, we thought they would come to see us even though they didn't really know what we were doing. Most international marketing people know the name Y&R and our reputation. Some of these visitors, we thought, would lead to assignments.

I didn't want to get involved in the details of getting our name up, but Vlasov insisted on showing me all the signatures and authorizations that were needed.

Finally, my impatience got the better of me. "You guys just buy the letters somewhere, go downstairs after hours, open the case, and put our name up." They did it, somewhat hesitantly, fearful of unknown consequences. There were no consequences. No one ever said anything to us. During the past seventy years, the working theory was "If it is not expressly permitted, then it is forbidden." In the West, the opposite has been true and innovation has followed.

At other times, I was forced to concede to long delays. In order for me to sign official documents, I had to have a signature card, just as in America. But the cards had to be signed in front of a notary, and there were only two notaries in all of Moscow that could issue proper authorization.

One day, Yuri Birasov, our financial director, and I made our way across town to get the cards notarized. We had thoroughly researched the process and knew exactly what we needed. Yuri was a bright man, docile, easy to talk to; we made small talk along the way.

"Things don't always go so smoothly," he warned. "We may have to wait in line."

"What a surprise," I kidded.

I was in a good mood. I knew we had all the appropriate papers, and I felt we were making good progress in getting the office open. Hiring Yuri also was one of the best decisions we had made. He was the third person in six months that we hired to fill our bookkeeper/financial director job. He was worth waiting for. The first one resigned because she couldn't take Vlasov's dictatorial management style. The second one took a couple of weeks of personal leave and never came back.

Mike was the first to interview Yuri. He met him while I was back in the States, making a speech at a *BusinessWeek* seminar on doing business in the Soviet Union. "You're not going to believe this guy I interviewed for our accountant job" were Mike's first words to me about Yuri over the long-distance lines. "I really like him, but I'm going to leave this decision up to you when you return."

Mike's unstated but implied concern was immediately apparent. Yuri was short and bent over because of a twisted spine. His skin was a pale gray, and he smoked one cigarette after another. He looked much older than his forty years. But the initial impression quickly passed once you started to talk with Yuri. His English was excellent; he had a wonderful sense of humor; he had traveled abroad and had a fine background working at the Chamber.

More important, I liked him. He was one of the few Soviets I could chat with and not feel as if he always had his guard up. He did, of course; he was just better at it. Yuri was also willing and trained to use accrual accounting methods. The other accountant and Vlasov both had told us accrual accounting was illegal.

After almost an hour's ride across town with Volodya, our driver, we arrived at the notaries' office. It was quite a decrepit old building, and the line for approvals snaked down the stairs and out the door. As a foreigner, I had the privilege of going to the head of the line, but that always made me so uncomfortable.

"Who am I to get in front of all these people?" I thought. "I'm not any better than they are."

The only time I regularly took advantage of that privilege

was at the airport, where I thought I might miss my flight if I didn't go to the front.

So, Yuri and I waited patiently as the line inched forward. Once inside, we slowly made our way up four flights of stairs, where we were offered seats in a shoddy, overheated room with dozens of other people.

It was so boring. "Patience, patience," I kept telling myself.

At least I had thought to bring along some work. One thing that never ceased to amaze me was that the Soviets seldom took anything with them to read when they knew they most likely would be standing in line for hours. They could be the best-read people in the world.

They just stand there with a blank stare on their faces. I'm not sure why, except that I think it has something to do with not wanting to open their lives to others. Sometimes they chat with one another, bitching about the long lines or wondering what's at the other end.

Yuri and I finally got to the front of the line and turned in our application. We were ready to sign in this huge ledger where all the signatures are kept on file. The offices looked like they were out of a Dickens novel, faded walls and tables piled high with huge ledgers where all the information is entered in longhand. Soviets take great pride in their penmanship and have beautiful handwriting.

"You don't have the right papers," Yuri translated the clerk's words. I had spent enough time in Moscow not to be surprised, but I certainly wasn't pleased. It was useless this time to object. So off we went with no signature cards, having wasted an entire morning.

We prepared another batch of papers, but it took several more trips over the next few weeks before we finally were allowed to sign the great ledgers. Once we waited for more than an hour while the two women took a coffee break. Each time we went, they'd tell us something else was not in order.

"Why not? What else has to be done?" The answers were never very clear. And they would give us different instructions each time. Eventually, the preemptive power of the makeup kit was brought to bear.

Around the office, my trips to the notary got to be a joke. At our Monday-morning staff meetings, we would discuss where we needed our cars for the week, and the financial director would say, "Well, we need one car to go to the notary." I would fume, and the staff would snicker as if to say, "He's learning." Eventually, even I could see the humor.

One reason we at Y&R picked Vneshtorgreklama as our Soviet partner was that as the only Soviet ad agency responsible for international advertising, we thought they would be able to facilitate some of the approvals and to gain access to influential people. Opening a business required dozens of permits and approvals. We needed a partner who knew the ropes and could operate through informal as well as formal channels to get certain jobs done.

"This is the premier international advertising agency in the Soviet Union," Alex Kroll had told me when he first outlined this job.

We thought Vneshtorgreklama could provide us with an "in." Any advertising that dealt with foreigners—either foreign companies advertising within the Soviet Union or Soviet organizations advertising outside the country—had to be handled by Vneshtorgreklama. When we were negotiating the deal, that seemed like a pretty powerful position to us.

At one of our first meetings with them, they explained how they operated under the Chamber of Commerce—an organization that we knew for sure was powerful within the Soviet hierarchy. But after the deal, as we began to set up the office, we were blocked at one path after another, and I started to question whether Vneshtorgreklama did have much influence.

I was frequently reminded of the first reaction of Mike Mears, the U.S. attaché, when I told him we were planning to open an advertising agency in Moscow. He had looked at me in open disbelief.

"An *advertising* agency?"

Once I started to analyze the role of communication in Soviet society, it occurred to me that it wasn't logical that Vneshtorgreklama would play an important role. Commercial communication was insignificant in a planned economy. Its sole purpose was to make sure the plan was carried out, as a propaganda tool to sell excess goods. Since demand for goods almost always outstripped supply, there was essentially no need for any mass commercial communication or persuasion.

A trip to the Soviet Union's most celebrated department store, GUM, was proof enough. The first time I went to browse, I was struck by its historical significance right on Red Square near Lenin's tomb and St. Basil's Cathedral. The GUM building is spectacular: a huge open structure covering a city block, with ornate interior bridges and crossovers, and a magnificent central fountain. Built in the late nineteenth century, it houses rows of stalls and shops on three floors.

Supposedly, GUM is the best stocked department store in the country; and I was told that hundreds of thousands of Soviets came from all over the Union to shop there every day. I guess that's why what I saw inside was so shocking. Many shelves were empty and those that were stocked carried poor merchandise with little variety. Where first you thought you had found a department filled with merchandise, you realized on second glance that the Soviets display one item many times over. In the shoe department, there might be rows and rows of shoes, but they would all be the same black lace-ups. No loafers; no wing tips. Just black lace-ups in only a few sizes.

The shoe department was typical, offering only one type of item, no choice of style — and sometimes no choice of size. It was at times like this that I understood why Mike Mears was so skeptical of whether we could achieve what we were trying to do. But he never said what I knew he must be thinking, "Why go to all this trouble if there's nothing to advertise?"

Bare shelves and long lines of desperate shoppers negating any reason whatsoever for advertising gave me a clearer understanding of why the organization responsible for commercial communication — international or no — would not be very influential.

This wasn't the only time I'd had to reexamine my initial thinking. I'm usually a pretty good judge of people. But my basic faith proved somewhat naive when it came to understanding how ingrained making something extra on the side was. Much of the initiative destroyed on the surface of the system showed itself beneath.

I was extremely impressed with Volodya, our driver — our own Steve McQueen, as Mike and I nicknamed him. The man with the penetrating blue eyes and sly grin. Volodya was so personable, and he was always eager to accommodate all our requests.

He made sure we knew what we should about car maintenance. On one of my first trips to Moscow on a dreary day, I spent an inordinate amount of time driving around. Although it was raining, I thought it was unusual to see several people in one day changing their windshield wipers.

"Oh, that's no coincidence," our driver said. "You have to remove your wiper blades and lock them up or they'll get stolen." I looked at him in amazement. Auto parts were in such short supply, and wiper blades took such abuse from the filthy slush of winter, that they were among the most precious parts, he told us. So, with the Fords we ordered from Helsinki, we made sure we had a good supply of extra wiper blades. Luckily, ours never disappeared.

More important, Volodya facilitated many goods through customs. He spent many an all-night vigil at Sheremetievo Airport waiting for shipments, and somehow got them delivered even when we were told that was impossible. In many ways, he was like the McQueen character, Hultz, in the classic movie *The Great Escape*.

Once, when I expected his task to be insurmountable, I said to him, "Just get me this shipment. I don't care how. And I don't want to know how. Just get it here." Even with that carte blanche from me, I was amazed when he came through.

Frankly, I thought he had a good opportunity to grow with our joint venture. His biggest challenge was to learn English, and we hoped he would take us up on our offer to pay for his lessons. Meanwhile, when he came to our early-morning training sessions, Natalie translated for him. With the language skills, he would be able to move into an office job. But Volodya never got around to starting lessons, and somehow, after his first few major contributions in facilitating the delivery of our furniture and supplies, he pulled away from us emotionally. I think he expected a bigger payoff when we got up and running, and once we *were* up and running, there was less need for what he does best.

He also let us down in keeping the cars clean. I'm a fanatic about clean cars, but this was a challenge in Moscow because the streets are always covered with grit and frequently muddy.

"Volodya, I want these cars washed every Friday evening

before you leave, so they'll be clean over the weekend when Mike and I drive them." I also wanted to start out the week with them looking good since we often drove clients around. But regardless of how many times I reminded Volodya, the cars weren't kept up to my standards. We parked them in the parking lot under the Mezh. One day, I saw that the caretakers had a car-wash business on the side.

"Can we work out a deal?" I asked them, after I got fed up bitching to Volodya about filthy autos.

"It'll cost you," they said.

At first they agreed to 20 rubles, but the price kept going up—40, 50 rubles. "Look, that's too much," I finally said. Then all they wanted was a can of Budweiser and a pack of Marlboros. So I ended up getting the cars cleaned in a barter deal. It was good for them and good for us.

Vlasov, who had brought Volodya in and been one of his biggest cheerleaders, turned against him.

"He's spending too much time in the cars," Vlasov grumbled.

"But that's his job, Vlasov," I reminded him. "He's supposed to be our driver." I was perplexed.

"Just too much time in those cars," he repeated.

It wasn't until months later that I learned what the real problem was and also how the "hidden economy," which I despised, worked against us. Vlasov had suspected—rightly so—that Volodya was using our staff cars to run a business on the side, taxiing people around Moscow. Once again Vlasov was embarrassed by his system.

But for Volodya, it was just the normal workings of the system. If we could beat the system in our way for us, why couldn't he use the system and our cars to make his life better?

4

EXPECT THE
UNEXPECTED

EVERY WEEK, I LOOKED FORWARD TO SATURDAYS. IT WAS THE ONLY time I could step back and laugh at the obstacles that blocked everything I was trying to do. This Saturday was going to be especially good. I was sure Mike Adams would win the free breakfast. Hands down.

Mike Mears, the commercial attaché at the American Embassy in Moscow, knew how important it was to inject a little laughter into each week. He'd survived in this city for several years, and he had become a master at keeping up morale. To the few American businessmen trying to operate here, he was our "scoutmaster" and "cheerleader" all rolled up in one.

He knew how tough it was to do business anywhere in the U.S.S.R. So he set up this contest that awarded a free breakfast to the guy who told the best story of the week.

Every week, most of the American business community would bring their wives and kids to the brunch at the U.S.

Embassy snack bar on Saturday mornings. This was one of the few American embassies in the world that gave access, limited though it was, to civilians. And it was certainly appreciated.

As my partner and I walked to the embassy this sunny, cold morning, I could hardly keep from laughing out loud. We passed by row upon row of nondescript concrete block buildings, some squat, some towering, all square and forbidding. The grand scale of Moscow's architecture reinforces the politics of the last seventy years. Massive buildings and broad expanses of city streets seem to have been conceived intentionally to make the individual feel small. The idea that the individual doesn't amount to much compared to "the people" is an important part of Communist doctrine, and the builders of Moscow fully succeeded in conveying that message to the masses.

No matter what neighborhood, the streets, like the washed-out gray and beige buildings, had a sameness about them — boulevards eight lanes wide, carrying little variety of autos. Most prevalent were the cheap Ladas and more sturdy black Volgas, the taxis and staff cars for the multitudes of middle-level bureaucracy, often seen reading a newspaper as their drivers whisked them through the traffic. Because of the lower percentage of cars owned privately in Moscow, there is a greater proportion of trucks than in the States: big, noisy, filthy, and belching inky smoke so black I often wondered if some of these mammoth vehicles were burning coal.

Occasionally a stodgy Zil limousine that I always thought looked more like a hearse than a luxury car would speed down the central lane reserved for VIPs. With blue lights flashing, the Soviet answer to the Lincoln stretch would zip through streets where cops sitting in small booths above the main intersections would stop traffic to allow the privileged — even in this classless society — to pass.

Along the sidewalks, Russians trudged purposefully, avoiding any acknowledgment of a familiar face and even eye contact with other passers-by. Yet this depressing scene couldn't dampen my spirits today.

As we rounded the last corner, I thought how much I appreciated Mike Mears. He had a special sensitivity to our needs—maybe because he wasn't a career civil servant and earlier had been in business for himself. One of his comments to me the first time I met him made me realize how much insight he had into this country where things just never seemed to go right.

"Gary," he said, "this is the only country where new buildings look old and new cars look used."

He understood that the business of feeding, clothing, housing, and transporting yourself here is a job in itself. In most countries, reliable room service is a given. So is a coffeeshop in any acceptable hotel. Laundry service is dependable, and most hotel concierges are invaluable in helping with such mundane but important chores as arranging transportation. But in Moscow, all the rules change.

There is no room service. You're lucky if your hotel has a restaurant and luckier still if it has food, and you have to haggle with the floor lady if you want laundry done. Finding transportation must be an art because there's nothing scientific about the way the taxis queue up.

Hovering near major hotels, taxi drivers usually huddle together outside their cars, most engrossed in conversation and smoking; it's difficult to get anyone's attention, and even more difficult to determine which driver is next in line. Then it's time to negotiate payment. Often, a pack of cigarettes—preferably Marlboro—is more acceptable than currency, hard or soft. All these normally routine activities drain your energy, until there's not much left to do the real business you're here for.

Mike Mears tried to make us forget the tough conditions by creating a warm environment at the embassy, a modern, efficient red-brick building that acted as the American community center as well as diplomatic headquarters. My partner and I were just passing the old U.S. Embassy building on the Inner Ring Road, the main traffic road around Moscow. The government still used this pre–World War II, European-style fortress for offices, even though the new, modern complex where we were headed had been built a few years ago. The office tower in the new red-brick complex a block away has remained empty because of the bugging of the office tower section in the much-publicized scandal involving a U.S. marine whose Russian girlfriend turned out to be KGB.

Just last week, I had to push through a crowd to get into the embassy offices. On one side was the usual line of bedraggled Soviets hoping to leave their country for the United States. Opposite them stood a sea of demonstrators picketing *against* the United States on some issue or another. Since today was Saturday, the offices were closed, so no crowds blocked the old stone facade from our view.

We walked up to the main entrance of the new complex, through the wrought-iron front gate guarded by a marine. Lovely red-brick Georgian-style townhouses where the top embassy personnel lived opened onto cobblestone streets, lined in the warm weather with colorful flower boxes, the only ones I'd seen in Moscow. Within the complex, we had access to modern facilities: a great gym, pool, snack bar, and chapel.

Several years after the bugging scandal, and a few months after Mike and I made our first trip to Moscow in October 1988, the American government was still trying to decide what to do with the bugged office tower. But here on Tchaikovsky Street was a place where we could relax with my new extended family. The men from Xerox, Combustion Engineering, Chiliwich, Polaroid, General Electric, Dresser, IBM, and Caterpillar usually came every week. When my wife Freddye moved here with me, I knew she would look forward to Saturdays, too. These hours were often the high point of the week, especially for families.

"Hey, we're right on time," I said to Mike. It was about 10:00 A.M.

"Yeah, everyone's just lining up for food."

Sometimes, others came early to play squash or swim. This time I was anxious to see the reaction to Mike's story. I stood in line, waiting to get to the steam tables of eggs and bacon, oatmeal and toast. If we were lucky, there would be biscuits and gravy, my favorite. The food brought back memories of my Navy days. They must have used the same cookbooks. In most installations, the cooks took great abuse; here they are the heroes.

There was the same old chipped beef on toast I remembered from OCS. Somehow, the name that we called it twenty-five years ago clear around the world—s.o.s, or shit on a shingle—had made its way to Moscow. After loading up my plate, I grabbed a chair and joined the crowd at the tables lined up end to end nearly across the room. We looked out of big glass sliding doors onto a plaza where the kids played in their snowsuits.

Mike was bursting to start in on his story. We had heard some wild tales before, mostly from the guys in the oil business. They often were out in the oil fields—out in the boonies, in towns we couldn't even find on a map. They'd come back with outrageous tales about hotels where you'd have to sleep two to a bed with a foul-smelling stranger, and stories of bad food or no food or no showers for a week. Or accommodations with outhouses.

I turned to Mike. "You're a shoo-in."

The story that he was to tell happened a few weeks earlier. Mike is a bear of a man with a genuine ready smile and a fabulous sense of humor. If he weren't a PR man, he'd have made a great talk-show host. He's a terrific storyteller.

Having had some time to embellish his story didn't hurt. We both watched Mike Mears work the crowd.

It wasn't a formal contest. There were no prepared stand-up presentations. Mears would just move around the tables, chat, and listen to story after story.

This week there must have been at least two dozen Americans for brunch. It was hard to tell how many were serious contenders.

Finally, Mears made his way down to our end of the table. "A few weeks earlier," Mike began, "Gary and I and another colleague, Claire, checked into the Intourist Hotel one Sunday night for a full week's stay. We were prepared for the typical eighteen-hour days that started before dawn and ended with business dinners…"

Mike didn't need to tell the Americans about Russian hotels. They knew from their own experiences. When you go to the Soviet Union, you can't just call up and make a reservation at the hotel of your choice. You have to go through a special organization, also called Intourist, that assigns you to a hotel. So, you never can tell which hotel you'll get until you're notified a day or two before you arrive.

Sometimes you get lucky and are sent to the "deluxe" Mezh, short for *Mezhdunarodnaya,* or Intercontinental. "Deluxe" means the phone works more often than not, and there is a TV in the room. Sometimes it works, too.

Most often, you get put up at another hotel, still officially classified as "first-class superior," but back home you'd classify it well below that. Usually, there's a shortage of hotel rooms in Moscow. So you take what you get, no questions asked.

After years of traveling all over the world and making reservations at the hotels I wanted, it was hard to get accustomed to being "assigned" to whatever was available. I felt like I was back in the service. For months after Mike and I started working in Moscow, we lived in one hotel after another before we could get apartments. For some reason — who knows why? — Mike and I were usually assigned to the National or the Intourist Hotel, two giant fortresses side by side on Marx Square. One was old, with lots of Old World charm and architecture, but badly neglected. The other was built relatively recently, but looked almost as ancient as a result of equal neglect.

This time it was the Intourist, the relatively modern one, that had a dark and grubby lobby because most of the fluorescent bulbs were missing. We dragged our luggage through the double set of doors to get inside. They tell you that the double doors are there to help keep the heat in the building. The real story is that this set-up requires you to enter single file and slowly, so that government security agents at the door have time to check and make sure you're not a Soviet. (Usually they can tell by the shoes.) Soviets aren't allowed in any of the better Soviet hotels without a special reason or appointment.

Same routine as usual. We walked through the dim, smoke-filled lobby to the long reception counter toward the left. Although at least a half dozen female clerks were chatting behind the high counter, it took several minutes of clearing our throats and looking impatient to get anyone's attention.

"Name?" one formidably formal middle-aged woman finally barked out.

"Burandt, Adams, and Montgomerie."

"Only one. One at a time." Never once did a clerk say, "Welcome to the Intourist," or, "How was your flight?" Never a pleasantry ever. Like most things Soviet, service was not critical to "success." The hotel was always full, and the clerks were paid the same even if it wasn't.

After the slow, manually handled check-in, she handed over room keys attached as usual to one-pound weights so we wouldn't leave the hotel with them. That was also a good way to know whether guests were in their rooms or whether the rooms were "available for inspection." On our own, since there were no bellmen, we took the creaky elevator to the eighth floor. I always hoped I'd be surprised one day with a good room. I never was.

I'd open the door. "No-o-o-o," I'd cringe as I looked in.

This time there was a tiny single bed, a scratched-up dresser, and at least a lamp that worked. Ugly dark floral wallpaper and the typical threadbare floral carpet. The TV was unplugged as usual. They're the biggest cause of fires in Russia, so they're kept unplugged except when you're using them.

On this trip, Mike's room was right next to mine. Claire Montgomerie, our attorney, was one floor above. It was late on Sunday when we checked in, so we went right to bed. The next day we were up and out early for a full day. After working late through a business dinner, we went back to our rooms. In the elevator, we all said, "Good night. See you at six A.M." Claire continued on the elevator, and Mike and I walked down the hall into our rooms.

About five minutes later, there was a knock on my door. It was Mike. "You've got to come see this. You're not going to believe it." He was shaking his head.

I go into his room, which is just as spartan as mine. He

directs me toward the bathroom. "I don't have a toilet any-more. It's gone," he says.

Sure enough, it *was* gone. Just a hole in the floor. There must be humor in all of this, but it was hard for us to laugh at that time of night. We were tired. Mike needed a toilet.

So we went to see the *dezhurnaya*, the floor lady. Every floor has one, supposedly to help, but in reality to watch. This one was a short, chubby, jovial woman. She could best be described as Danny DeVito in drag.

Mike complained about the missing toilet. And she wasn't even surprised. I guess we weren't, either. We'd been in Moscow long enough—several months since we had started traveling back and forth from the States—to expect the unex-pected.

The floor lady told him in Russian, "I'm terribly sorry. There was a crack in the bowl and it had to be replaced. They thought they could get another one the same day."

Mike graciously told her he'd use my toilet since I was just next door. And she promised it would be taken care of the next day.

Next night. Back late again. "Good night, see you in the morning." Five minutes later, there was Mike at my door again, looking annoyed. I grinned. "Still gone?" He nodded.

"But there's an improvement," he said with a mock groan. "They left me a plastic bucket."

We go to the floor lady again. She says, "Mr. Adams, I'll get that taken care of for you first thing tomorrow. I'm going to write them up. Report them. This is terrible. Don't worry. I'll take care of it."

So off we went to bed. Next night, same situation. By now, it had become a *cause célèbre*, and even before I went to my room I trekked into Mike's with him—Claire came to inspect, too. Still no toilet. She got back on the elevator laughing all the way down the hall. That night we couldn't find the *dezhurnaya*.

By now, everyone within earshot in the embassy snack bar is listening to Mike's story and chuckling. Mike's in his glory.

"That night, after I'm sound asleep," Mike continues, "there's a knock on my door. I look at my watch. It's one A.M. I drag myself out of bed, open the door, and there's this cherubic little face, a one-hundred-eighty-pound compact little woman, beaming up at me. '*Kak-de-la, kak-de-la* [How are you? How are you?],' she sings out. It was the *dezhurnaya*. She came to find out if my toilet was replaced."

The way Mike tells it he didn't even make any pretense of exchanging pleasantries. He didn't slam the door in her face, but he felt like it. In any case, our little game of betting on when the missing toilet would return lasted the whole week. Mike never got his toilet.

Now, three weeks later, he could laugh about it. "I swear this whole incident happened because when I checked into my room, I played electrician," Mike said, thinking back. "Not a single light worked in my room. So I whipped out my trusty Swiss Army knife and corrected some wiring, meanwhile grumbling and swearing out loud that nothing in this country works right."

"So I guess they showed you," someone listening to Mike's story suggested.

"It's a lesson I won't forget." Mike laughed.

But he didn't win the brunch prize that Saturday. A story told by a sales rep who worked for Xerox was even more unbelievable.

Earlier that week, the rep was trying to sell some copiers in a small town near Tashkent. It's hot, dusty, dry country thousands of miles southeast of Moscow. He was sitting at a little outdoor café midday in a town square having coffee. Wearing his Western clothes in that Muslim region where robes are more common attire was a clear signal that he was a foreigner.

Suddenly, the sales rep sees an odd character approaching him from across the square. It was hot, and the townspeople were taking life easy, moving slowly. This tall, dark-complexioned man in strange garb glides slowly toward him, taking huge, methodical strides. The Xerox guy thinks he must be imagining things. But no. Some man wearing a brightly colored, flowing, hooded robe really is approaching.

His arms are outstretched and on them are perched three brown falcons, wearing the leather hoods that are the mark of prized hunting birds. As he gets closer to the sales rep, the character's massive appearance is even more impressive.

He comes within inches and stands right over our Xerox friend, peering down at him, blocking out the sun.

His voice booms out: "Are you ... Xerox Man?"

Meekly, the sales rep replies, "Uh-huh."

In broken but clearly understandable English, the strange character says, "I trade you ... I trade you ... three falcons for copy machine."

That wasn't exactly the deal our Xerox friend was trying to make, but he did win the brunch prize that week. It seems that bad hotel stories like Mike's come cheap.

As if the hotel hadn't done enough damage to Mike's psyche, there's a postscript. He and I made elaborate plans to demand a price break on the hotel room. It would seem reasonable not to pay full price for a room without a toilet. Our plane was scheduled to leave at the crack of dawn on Friday, and Mike overslept. That was pretty unusual for him. By the time he was ready to leave, it was late, and we knew if we stopped to argue, we'd probably miss our plane and not get another for several days. It wasn't worth a fight.

I asked Mike, "How could you oversleep?"

With a look of total helplessness, he said, "The hotel forgot to give me my wake-up call."

I'd like to say that Mike's missing toilet mystery was the most trying episode during the year and a half I spent in Moscow, when we set up and opened Young & Rubicam's joint venture in the Soviet Union, but it wasn't. Nothing in my career had prepared me for this. And everything had prepared me for it. I know how to create good advertising. I know how to run an office. I had worked in foreign countries enough to be able to function effectively within different cultures. As a young public affairs naval officer in Japan twenty-five years ago, I had to deal with a highly charged issue: nuclear-powered submarines. The subs would come into port, and there would be thousands of demonstrators in the streets. Those were tense times, but there was a difference. I had good translators I could depend on, phones that worked, taxis at a moment's notice, and back-up support. Here in the Soviet Union, Mike and I had to rely on each other, common sense, and ingenuity. Certainly, we had the support of Kroll and Y&R, but they were a long way away.

Once, before our office cars arrived, some of our Soviet staff and I were making calls on clients. Taxis were usually plentiful but we had to make lots of stops and wanted our own car.

Valery Fedorov, one of our Soviet account directors, offered: "Let me drive."

I figured even though his Lada—a Soviet-made sixties Fiat—had seen better days, it was better than hailing taxis. Not many Muscovites are lucky enough to have their own car. Fedorov probably got his because he was a wheeler/dealer par excellence. We hired him partly because he knew his way around in Moscow.

I'd ask Fedorov, "Can you get us tickets to the circus for a client?" Next day there they were on my desk.

"How about a meeting with the TV administration people?" I'd say to him.

Somehow he'd get it set up after I'd been trying unsuccessfully for days. A real fixer was Fedorov. And he looked the part. His expression was always masked so you could never tell what he was up to. He wore better-quality suits than most of our staff, but they always looked as if they needed pressing. When Mike and I ended up giving the staff code-names (that's a story in itself for later), Fedorov's was "Dom" because Mike and I knew a ticket "fixer" back in Chicago named Dom.

Taller than I am, Fedorov was probably more than six feet, but didn't look it because he always slumped over and never seemed to walk with any great purpose. He had dark, longish hair, parted on the left side, and a sallow complexion. Like many Soviets, he was a heavy smoker. He always gave off the vibes that he was doing us a favor by working for us, unlike the rest of the enthusiastic staff. This time, he was proud that he could offer to drive us in his own car.

By American standards, it was almost ready for the junkheap; even by Soviet standards, it was in bad shape. You could see places where it was held together with wire. There were holes in the floor, so that as you drove along, you could see straight through to the street beneath. It was hard to tell whether the original exterior was reddish-orange or whether that came from all the rust.

Moscow isn't kind to autos. Hard winters, few repair shops, and a scarcity of spare parts make for lots of rusty, noisy vehicles on the streets. Most, like Fedorov's, were low-price Ladas, not that well made to begin with. Every so often you'd see larger, better-made Volgas or a few Western Volvos or Mercedes, which always belonged to the expatriate or diplomatic community. Fedorov made matters worse by driving like Parnelli Jones, whipping around corners on two wheels, winding out the engine in each gear.

Still, I appreciated his offer to drive. We started out, but after just a few blocks the car would start to tilt toward the right and rock back and forth.

"It's time to get out and pump," Fedorov said.

The right rear tire had a slow leak. It'd been there for months, but even Fedorov the Fixer didn't have enough pull to get that tire fixed. It's not like in America. You can't just stop at a service station. There are no service stations, and it sometimes takes months to find someone with the materials to fix a leaky tire.

So, every few blocks we'd have to get out and pump. With a bicycle pump. Drive several blocks. Stop again. Pump.

I said, "This Moscow ad agency is a fifty-fifty venture. I suppose I should do my part and pump up the tire half the time."

It was a hot June day, and we were dressed in three-piece suits.

"No, no, no." Federov protested, embarrassed.

Finally, I insisted. "I'm riding in the car, too. There's no reason I can't pump."

Here I am, the CEO of the first Western ad agency in Moscow, drenched in sweat from pumping up a leaky tire on Kalinin Prospekt, one of the best-known boulevards in downtown Moscow. My colleagues back home should have a picture of this.

I got so tickled that I started laughing out loud.

Vladimir Vlasov, my Soviet counterpart, was with us. He

glared at me as I laughed. Vlasov wouldn't pump; it was beneath his station.

"You're mocking us." He was terribly embarrassed that his system once again was being exposed as inadequate.

A month before, Vlasov had made his first business trip to America to visit several Y&R agencies. I met him and Yuri Pashin, the number-two Soviet in the venture who went with him, at Kennedy Airport in a limo. I can imagine he must have been thinking how when he was in my country, he was sitting there in that big fancy car with a phone, TV, and fully stocked bar being driven to the Grand Hyatt Hotel in midtown New York. Here, in his country, I was pumping tires just to get to an appointment at the local TV station.

"You're laughing at us," he repeated.

"Vladimir," I said, "this would be funny no matter what country we were in. Lighten up."

Vlasov was from the old school. A man of about sixty, he was formal and stiff and did everything by the book—a typical old Bolshevik, motivated by fear and pride. It was obvious he was far more concerned about how bad his system looked than I was. I had already accepted that as a fact and gotten beyond it. I knew his *system* was bad, not the people. I was just trying to figure out how to cope with it. He wasn't so forgiving.

Most of the time, I tried hard to treat the staff as I would Y&R staffers in any other country. I would explain to them why I did things a certain way so that they would understand. After all, part of my responsibility to the Soviet staffers as the American partner was to train them in how to do business and communications Western style.

Although I wanted to be considerate of their feelings, I felt it was important not to be overly sensitive just because I was working in a totally different environment. If Mike and I didn't cause change, there would be no improvement.

Sometimes, however, all my good intentions backfired. Sometimes, my indignation at the way their system worked — or didn't work — caused more trouble than I bargained for. After several months of traveling back and forth to Moscow enduring Vlasov's seeming ineffectualness, I took what for me was the pretty drastic step of going over his head. I thought long and hard about how to make my point without naming names and placing any blame.

It happened when I came back to Moscow after a grueling few weeks of drumming up client business in the United States. While I was doing that, Vlasov was supposed to be finding apartments for Mike and me, getting multiple-entry visas for us and our families, and obtaining bids for office improvements. There was a delicate balance we had to achieve in starting up the office and getting clients; the timing had to be such that one didn't get too far ahead of the other. So, Vlasov and I had to be in synch. But while I was gone, nothing Vlasov was supposed to be working on had been taken care of. On the surface, he didn't seem concerned about it at all. I was furious.

"Difficult, very difficult," was the most I could pull out of him when I asked why nothing had been done.

"We're going to start making check-off lists," I told him. If this was an insult, too bad. But even that didn't help things move along much faster.

"What about item number four?" I'd ask him.

"The person that could authorize it was out sick," he'd tell me.

"And item number seven?"

"That person was away."

It's true that the Soviets have no back-up systems. If someone is away or ill, the work piles up on their desk, and no one else has the authority or inclination to cover for them. It's not unusual for workers to be absent from their jobs to stand in long lines for, say, soap, if a shipment has just come in. Their absence is overlooked as long as they bring back enough bars for their supervisor and others.

Later I figured out that Vlasov was too proud simply to admit that his system was inefficient. Even though it wasn't a personal failure on his part, he was the representative, and it was *his* system.

I finally got so frustrated that I made an appointment with the number-two man at the U.S.S.R. Chamber of Commerce, Vladimir Golanov. He suggested lunch for the four of us— himself, Vlasov, Mike, and me. Golanov was a powerful man. As the number-two person, he ran day-to-day operations of the Chamber. And Gorbachev was relying on the Chamber to develop joint ventures between Soviet and foreign companies, in the hope of fueling the country's changing economy.

The Socialist political system had failed to deliver promised benefits; left unchecked, the discontent of the people could threaten the country's stability. Gorbachev understood that he must somehow bring in basic consumer goods that people in the West take for granted—paper, food, tobacco, shoes, cosmetics. Joint ventures with Western companies would provide capital and know-how that could be matched by the Soviets' facilities and labor to produce those goods.

This was a top-priority mission of the Chamber of Commerce, the organization overseeing our joint venture partner. So, making sure our venture was progressing was important to Golanov, since ours in turn could attract others.

He was a bright, dedicated man, who always seemed tired. I liked him. He spoke English fairly well, but better French. He loved France and fortunately got a posting there later.

We got down to business after a quick exchange of pleasantries. "This joint venture is not going to get off the ground at the rate we're going," I told him flatly. "We need apartments; we need usable office space; we need visas." I went through the laundry list, careful not to point fingers at any one person in particular.

He listened carefully, asked a few questions, and his aide wrote everything down. When I had finished, he turned to Vlasov. What followed was a loud, unpleasant exchange between the two of them. Since it was in Russian, I didn't know whether Vlasov or I was being done in. But I could tell someone was.

All Golanov said to Mike and me was that he was sorry we were having problems and he'd see what he could do.

"That was the most embarrassing public dressing down I've ever seen," Mike said after lunch. "He thoroughly blasted Vlasov and told him he'd better get his shit together." Mike's knowledge of Russian came in handy.

"I certainly didn't expect such a reaction. At least not in front of us," I allowed.

Neither of us had ever seen such a public humiliation in all our years in business, and I hoped it wouldn't hurt our already strained relationship with Vlasov. What really mattered, though, was whether it helped get our joint venture off the ground. Only time would tell.

5

DRUMMIMG UP
BUSINESS

I COULD SEE PEOPLE ON THE STREET WATCHING ME, PUZZLED, AS I whistled a cheerful tune and jauntily strode along the sidewalk. The bounce in my step and smile on my face were in sharp contrast to the more serious mood and somber expression Russians normally wear in public, especially on cold dreary winter days like this. I was bringing good news to the staff, and I couldn't hide my delight. We had our first client—Johnson & Johnson, a fine one. It was déjà vu since J&J was one of Y&R's first clients in New York many years ago.

I had just finished a phone conversation with Dr. Heinz Schmidt, the J&J man in charge of o.b. tampons, a J&J brand, in Eastern Europe and China.

"We want you to help introduce o.b. tampons to the Soviet Union," he said.

Although a tough assignment, it was a welcome one. Most women fashioned something at home out of rags for sanitary protection. Very few had ever heard of tampons. Less than

15 percent of Soviet women knew that any manufactured external or internal sanitary protection products existed. Usually, tampons follow the introduction of external pads in a country. But here, because cotton, the basic material in tampons, was prevalent, and cellulose, the main material in pads, wasn't, tampons made more sense.

The Russians were a prudish people.

"Mike, this won't be an easy first assignment," I confessed when I phoned my partner about the win.

"It wouldn't be easy even if it weren't the first, but it will be a big challenge. It'll give us a chance to see which of our staff are up to the tough ones."

And it *was* good for morale. Theirs and mine. It was January 1989—three months after my first trip to Moscow. At this point we didn't have an office. I didn't have an apartment. Nor did Mike. We didn't even have a final joint venture agreement. But we had a client, and we would do our best for them. Of that I was certain.

Reaction among the staff was predictable. "Well, guys," I told them first off as we gathered in a borrowed conference room at the Mezh Hotel. "We have won our first client, so we'll be doing more than just setting up the office. We'll be doing some billable work."

"We have to get set up first." Vlasov was skeptical. "We're not prepared to handle clients yet."

"We'll be earning hard currency, Vladimir. It will pay for some of our expenses." Those were the magic words to convince him.

Roman, wearing the warm grin I was growing accustomed to, was enthusiastic and looked forward to the challenge. "I'd like to work on that assignment," he volunteered. Yuri Pashin, Vlasov's number-two man, was just Pashin, accepting almost any news—good or bad—with equanimity. Willing to work on any assignment, he was eager to please.

With his blond hair and casual style, Pashin made a good foil to Vlasov's formal demeanor. He didn't have the skills and management discipline that we would have sought under other circumstances, but I attributed that to his lack of exposure. A quick study, he was much more cooperative than Vlasov and willing to admit he was not wise in the ways of business.

We had worked hard to land the J&J business. The company's relationship with Y&R was close, and as soon as they heard we were opening, they wanted to see what we could do for them.

"The J&J people are coming in to brief us on their Soviet plans," our New York client services director told me even before I made my first trip. "They want to meet you."

I was at a terrible disadvantage: The guy coming in spent 60 percent of his time in the Eastern bloc. This year, he'd already been in Moscow eight times. My first impression of Bill Dearstyne was that he's a modern-day Abe Lincoln, tall, lean, and imposing. When he talked, you could tell he was a no-nonsense sort of guy.

"You know, Bill, I'm going to learn a lot more from this conversation than you are from me." I figured honesty was the best policy, that Dearstyne didn't appear to be the type to suffer fools and that if I tried to b.s. him, it would only fail. Anyway, it's not my style.

"I don't know much yet. But we're going to be in Moscow soon, we're going to learn quickly, and we're going to offer the services that you need," I told him.

I think he appreciated my straightforwardness at that first meeting.

"I like what I'm hearing," he told me. "But I'm still talking to other agencies, even though Y&R/Sovero is high on my list." I wondered who the others could be, since no one else was opening an outpost yet.

During one of my frequent trips to Moscow, he called to say he was in town and asked if we could meet that same day. Visiting Western businessmen always pack every day with appointments so that they only have to stay a short time. Moscow doesn't rank very high as a fun or productive place for traveling executives.

I immediately turned to Vlasov. "I hope you're free at four today." This would be the first time Vlasov and I together met with a prospect. "We're going to meet with Johnson & Johnson."

Vlasov tried not to show his nervousness. "What do I do? What do I say?" But a slight quiver of his mouth betrayed him.

"J&J has been a client of Y&R for years. They know our philosophy and our work. We'll need to discuss what we can do for them specifically in this market," I told him.

I wanted Vlasov along because I wanted Dearstyne to see we were indeed in serious negotiations, making good progress with our joint venture and in developing a competent Soviet staff.

Vlasov and I met Dearstyne and a couple of his staff in the Mezh lobby "under the clock," a common meeting place for Westerners. It was very noisy. I looked around. Pockets of business people were chatting, some in English, some in Russian, still others in other languages. There aren't many places to sit in the Mezh lobby, and no place secluded enough to have a private chat.

"I have a suite upstairs. Let's go there where it's quiet," Dearstyne suggested, after we said our hellos.

Vlasov got visibly more nervous and uncomfortable. It took him a few minutes to control the quiver and get back the fixed stern look he usually wore. Later I learned that under the old rules he wasn't supposed to be the only Soviet meeting with foreigners in a hotel room with the door closed.

But he came without any comment. I noticed that he didn't carry a briefcase. I wondered how he planned to take any notes of the meeting. What if the client gave us an assignment or asked for information? Both he and I had a lot to learn about each other.

"Would you like a beer?" Dearstyne said cheerfully as we shed our suit jackets and settled comfortably on the couch. Even with that, Vlasov just couldn't relax. He sat stiffly on the edge of the sofa—very formal, still wearing his jacket buttoned—as he tried to look around inconspicuously at what to him was quite a luxurious suite. To me it was comparable to a badly maintained Motel 6. Drab couch, dark florals; preponderance of brown.

Dearstyne briefed us on what products he hoped to introduce: tampons and baby products if all went well on the joint venture that was in negotiation with a cotton-processing plant in Soviet Georgia.

After about half an hour, Vlasov could sit still no longer. "You know," he said, "business in general operates differently here." Then he pontificated for a good fifteen minutes on a topic mostly irrelevant to our meeting. Dearstyne nodded politely, and Vlasov ended up by trying to convince Dearstyne that a rooftop neon sign would be a good way to introduce the tampons.

"I don't think that's what we have in mind for right now, but thank you for your thoughts, Vladimir," Dearstyne said.

As I bid Dearstyne goodbye, he took me aside and said, "You're going to have your hands full with him," gesturing toward Vlasov.

That night in the hotel, I confided in Mike. "It was quite a performance from Vlasov." I applauded my Soviet counter-part's spirit—his efforts to show he could make a contribu-tion—but neon signs for tampons weren't my idea of a good fit.

"An A for effort?" Mike wanted to give him the benefit of the doubt.

"I guess."

Dearstyne and I continued to meet whenever we were in the same city. We hit it off well. He seemed to admire my doggedness. He had been working in this part of the world for a couple of years, and after many more months' effort than Y&R still didn't have his business up and running. When I told him I planned to have my office intact before the American Trade Council Exhibition in October, in just nine months, he laughed.

"You just wait and see," I challenged. "It will look like a Y&R office anywhere."

"I bet you a dinner anywhere in Moscow that you won't," Dearstyne said in earnest.

"That's a deal, my friend." We shook on it.

Later, when I showed off the office to him that fall, he stuck out his hand. "Congratulations. I never thought you'd do it. I owe you a dinner." It was a proud moment for me.

It was through Dearstyne that I met Dr. Schmidt, the J&J tampon king of the world. A sparkling-eyed, portly German gentleman in his sixties, Dr. Schmidt had no delusions about how difficult introducing tampons to the Soviets would be.

I was the naive one. My staff would have to take a crash course in market research—something that didn't occur to me at first—before we could even start on the project.

"The first step," I told the staff, "is to research the market." The blank stares on their faces told me no one knew what a usage and awareness study was. So I had to step back and say, this is the information we want—what women use for sanitary protection now, and how many are aware of the product category and any brand names — and here's how you organize the research. I had plans to teach market research in regularly scheduled training sessions, but we hadn't started that yet because we didn't have our office. We decided to use an outside research firm to actually conduct the research, but I wanted the staff to learn about market research also.

So much of the training was on the job, learning as we worked. I sat down and explained to them that they should think about our clients' customers and develop a profile in their minds about these prospects.

In order to do effective advertising, you must know who you're talking to and what the customer thinks and feels. A good profile can be developed through demographics: sex, age, income, where people live, country, city, their media habits. But you also need to know psychographics. Are they achievers? Conservative, risk takers, followers? The staff had a hard time understanding some of this. The idea, first, that within a society people could be vastly different, and second, that they could be categorized wasn't easy for them to comprehend.

The hardest concept to teach was choice. They'd never had much of that either in the marketplace or in their political system.

"Focus groups!" Mike scoffed. He knew the Soviets better than I. "We're going to have enough trouble getting women to be honest with us about anything here, much less talking about their menstrual practices." So we ended up hiring a Soviet social research firm to do one-on-one private interviews.

Vlasov's behavior was predictable. Throughout the project, he could hardly bring himself to say the word "tampons," he was so embarrassed. Once Mike and I felt especially mischievous and sat around the conference table with a box, flipping it around and opening it up. We thought Vlasov was going to crawl under the table. J&J gave us a plastic demonstration model of the female pelvis, complete with all cutaway organs. Vlasov made sure that the model was kept locked from view.

I had been introduced to the Soviet social research group through the famous Gallup research people in the States, and I went to discuss our project with their very bright and likable director. I was getting accustomed to offices like his, dark, drab, and dingy. He was working on the saddest PC I'd ever seen. The director himself looked awful.

"I haven't had a night's sleep in days," he told me. He was working on the first overnight political polling ever done in the Soviet Union. The first-ever Congress of People's Delegates was in session.

Gorbachev was giving speeches almost daily and wanted to know how the people were reacting. I couldn't help thinking: "Here in this land where democracy is only beginning, they've raced ahead to do overnight polling."

Natalie Belova, our rapidly rising receptionist/secretary, became the agency's research project director for tampons. She briefed the research firm which did the actual interviews by having their people travel to cities in four different republics. We translated instructions into Russian, and the researchers gave out o.b. tampon samples to about twenty-five women in each city. In the interviews, they explained what the product was, how to use it, and noted the initial reactions of the panelists.

In the southernmost cities, a less developed part of the country, there was less willingness to participate. Some of the reaction was "That part of my body belongs to my husband, and he wouldn't like that."

Two months later, the researchers went back to the women and interviewed them about their experience with the product, asked them how much they would pay for it, and whether the instructions and printed materials were written clearly. Routine market research in America; a remarkable accomplishment in this country.

Even after we got the results of our research, I wasn't sure of the accuracy. The problem in the Soviet Union is that people are so accustomed to responding to questions with answers they think the questioner wants to hear rather than with the truth that you're never sure about the accuracy of data. Even government records are poor because managers are so used to lying about their production to meet their five-year quotas. Records and files are doctored by people whose jobs and even lives are on the line.

We recommended to our client that they learn from Tampax's experiences. Tambrands knew the Soviet Union was a big market. They raced in to be first, but they made a mistake trying to supply the whole country from one factory in the Ukraine. As a result, consumers could never be assured of an adequate supply. A shipment would show up at a store; a line would form. Women would stand for three hours, buy ten boxes each, stash them under their beds, and hope they could find them again before they ran out. Tampax sold 1 million boxes of tampons the first three days on the market. A great initial success, but production simply couldn't keep up with demand.

J&J wouldn't be far behind, but we recommended that they sell only in Moscow at first, and that they designate a leading drugstore in each of the city's districts.

"Keep those stores supplied so that women are assured the product will be there when they want to buy it. They will appreciate reliability, and you will gain their confidence—and gratitude—by fulfilling your promises," we advised Dr. Schmidt.

Our feeling was that the Russians would be extremely loyal to a company that could provide adequate regular supplies. Natalie and Roman were invaluable in helping us think this through. "All we know about advertising here is that it's government propaganda. Since no one knows what's true and what's not, people tend to disregard all messages," Natalie said.

On one point she was quite insistent: "It's very important not to overpromise." Once Natalie felt she had gained our confidence, she was quite vocal and set herself up as the expert spokesperson for the Russian consumer, especially the women. She stood erect and proud as she voiced her strong opinions.

Research indicated not unexpectedly that once women understood the product, it would be quickly accepted. In America, such favorable research results would mean we would introduce nationally without test markets and regional rollout and with lots of advertising support. In the Soviet Union, limited manufacturing capacity and a general lack of knowledge about sanitary protection products prompted us to recommend a different kind of introductory program.

We also were charged by J&J to revise the packaging, so we hired a famous Soviet graphic artist who produced several examples. We chose the one closest to international branding and kept the o.b. name. While the name didn't have the same significance that it had in the West, the letters were a nice combination of sound.

To encourage trial, J&J planned to charge 1 ruble for 10 tampons; but when women said up to 5 rubles was not unreasonable at all, based on the great convenience, J&J planned to raise the price.

The proposed advertising was not promotional or competitive but educational. It told what the product was, how to use it, assured women that it was safe, and explained where to buy it.

We proposed developing educational programs to send to gynecological clinics and schools, and training programs for sales reps for when they called on gynecologists and obstetricians. Our proposal covered all aspects of introduction, and J&J loved it.

We planned to make Dr. Schmidt a TV personality by putting him on talk shows and having him featured in health magazines.

"I wish all our agencies were as good as this one," Dr. Schmidt said to Roman and Natalie. We all beamed. To reward the account team, he invited those who had worked on the project out to dinner at the Savoy, a restaurant in a beautifully restored old hotel. Tall ceilings, sparkling bright chandeliers—the grandeur of the Czars. The hotel had been restored in 1989 by the Finns and operated as a joint venture between Finnair and Mosoviet, the city council. Only travelers on Finnair could stay in the Savoy, a practice that probably wouldn't be allowed in most countries. But in the Soviet Union, somehow such conventions go unrecognized.

This was the first time any of the Soviets had been to the hotel. Natalie's pride in her government for making sure the restoration was done properly was quite evident. A history buff, she took in everything around her. It would probably be many years—if ever—before she was in this very expensive, elegant restaurant again.

Although her English was excellent, she hadn't heard of many of the items on the menu—prawns and kiwi, for example—and she grew frustrated with all the choices because she wanted to taste everything. For once in Moscow, the restaurant could fill any order on the menu. Freddye sat next to Natalie and guided her through. As she sampled the fish mousse appetizer she finally chose, she savored every bite. It was a delight to watch her expression change from one of anticipation to satisfaction. Every course was a delicacy for her, straight through to the exotic fresh fruit she selected for dessert.

When the Russians entertained, it was usually at lunch, because lunch is less expensive than dinner (even though the menu is often the same), and the Soviets would take us to a place where they could spend their rubles, usually the Ukraine Hotel dining room. It was not too far from the office, near the U.S.-U.S.S.R. Chamber of Commerce. I'm sure it was embarrassing for them, but we all understood and made the best of it.

Still, it was a hassle, because we'd have to find a taxi if our cars were busy, and that meant going through the routine of bargaining. Most businessmen learned that cigarettes, airline amenity kits, pens, pocketknives, and lighters could buy services faster than money. I always carried a carton of Marlboros in my briefcase. (Once I got four shirts washed and pressed at my hotel for a disposable headphone set from Pan Am.)

Then we'd get to the restaurant, and despite a menu that sounded enticing, the choices were generally limited to fish, meat, or perhaps chicken. No choice of preparation.

As time went on, much better cooperative restaurants began to open. You could spend hours trying to find out their phone numbers—there are no public phone directories in Moscow—and more time finding one that wasn't booked. They were expensive. They often required payment in hard currency, and it wasn't unusual to pay $100 per person for a meal. But tonight at the Savoy, thanks to Dr. Schmidt, was not a time to think of all that.

We finished developing the J&J materials. We were ready. Now it was up to the J&J people to sign their joint venture with the factory in Soviet Georgia to get production going. The project lingered at this stage and was still unsigned when I left

Moscow. Yet the pattern of frustration at not being able to see any results in the marketplace was not uncommon.

Our good work led to other J&J assignments: dental floss, toothpaste, and baby products. We conducted some research with baby products that also involved in-home sampling. The mothers loved us because they enjoyed the lotion, powder, and oil, and that classic J&J smell just as much as American mothers do. We did another sampling project for Heinz baby food. As the shipments came in from the West, we stacked cases and cases of baby food in every empty space in the office under lock and key until we could ship them out to the field. The sampling program was a roaring success, but we weren't sure how much baby food made it to the baby's stomach because the adults loved the taste and knew it was a relatively inexpensive source of very good nutrition.

As rewarding as our work was, there was a downside on almost every project. We readied introductory assignments and they never got off the ground because our clients' joint ventures got bogged down. As the negotiations dragged on, their initial enthusiasm waned, and many began to worry about what they would do with so many millions of virtually worthless rubles. How do you convert them into something useful to shareholders back home?

One project that moved quickly at first was our work with Colgate toothpaste. With the resources of a colleague, Lumi Sava, we helped Colgate find a joint venture partner in the Ukraine to build a toothpaste factory. Our troubles began with an outdoor sign on Gorky Street that we wanted to use for Y&R's famous poster showing a tube of toothpaste squeezing the smile onto a face.

When Colgate's engineers took a look at the sign site, they were appalled. "No way this building will hold our sign. It will fall through the roof. You'll have to rebuild the roof or find another site." Neither option was such an easy task.

"And if you use this site, the power to light the sign isn't adequate." Nothing is easy in this town.

When McDonald's opened its first fast-food restaurant in Moscow, Coca-Cola asked us to develop a program to support the opening. McDonald's is Coke's biggest customer. We created banners to hang across Gorky Street (the main shopping strip) and other major thoroughfares, and arranged to show Coca-Cola commercials on a huge electronic billboard on Kalinin Prospekt. Why this unsophisticated city had such a high-tech sign was just another of those inexplicable anomalies, but we were glad to be able to use it.

The day before we were supposed to hang the banners, I got a call from Coke. "Mike, we've got to hold off. The people living near the restaurant are afraid of the crowds and litter from the hamburgers. McDonald's has decided not to do any promotion because they've already gotten so much publicity, and they'd prefer that we don't hang the banners."

Mike called the Mosgoroformlenije, the city design directorate that "rented" us the space. "Look, I'm sorry we're canceling at the last minute," he told the director. "So we'll pay you a 25 percent cancellation penalty."

"Everyone is planning to see those signs up. You can't cancel. You must hang them!" the director pleaded.

"We're sorry, Mr. Kliushkin. The client doesn't want them up."

"I'm sending over my representative to get the signs. They must go up."

Luckily, we had the banners in the trunk of one of our cars, not at the painting firm where he sent his men.

For Mr. Kliushkin, those banners were a matter of saving face. He was so happy to get some hard currency from renting the space that he had bragged of his accomplishment to everyone in city government. When we canceled, he knew he'd be embarrassed, and he was as much concerned about that as he was about collecting the money.

The naivete of the Soviets in business hit me once again. He didn't understand that his business and my business and Coca-Cola's business were about customer satisfaction. We were Kliushkin's customer; Coke was ours and McDonald's was Coke's. If those signs had gone up against our wishes, there would have been customer dissatisfaction right down the line. Actually, it would have been more than dissatisfaction; it could have meant real trouble.

The electronic billboard did light up at the end of January 1990 just as McDonald's opened its store — and with great fanfare. We ran six great musical commercials every ten minutes, and the giant electronic board on the street drew shoppers out of stores and stopped traffic. The commercials weren't ours. They were Coke's regular international spots, created and produced by McCann-Erickson, and as big a hit in Moscow as elsewhere around the world.

On the first evening, I drove by to make sure everything went off as planned. The expressions on the face of the usually expressionless Russians were priceless. They smiled and laughed, an animation they would have been embarrassed about. I was so pleased. These little rewards made this job all worthwhile.

But as the commercials continued to run, I said to Freddye, "Uh-oh, they're running that Santa commercial." It was after Christmas and we didn't think a Christmas commercial was appropriate, especially in this supposedly atheist society — and a month after Christmas.

Fuming, I phoned Mike. "They're running the Santa commercial. What happened?"

"Damn. Something always gets fouled up!"

After checking around, he called me back. "You're not going to believe this. The commercials are shown manually, and the guy running them likes the Santa commercial. He decided it should run—to hell with what the client wants."

I just shook my head. What an attitude. There were some things I would never get used to.

Many small projects kept us busy. There were some industrial assignments for companies such as General Electric; and we helped Baskin-Robbins to open a store on Gorky Street, and Murjani to launch a frequent buyers' club. We tried to get something going with IBM, Kodak, Du Pont, and Adidas, but nothing significant materialized while I was there.

Right after we got J&J, we landed another piece of business, Universal International Pictures (UIP), a British company that wanted to distribute western movies in the U.S.S.R.

There was a huge black market in videotapes of western movies, but so far no regular showings in the many movie theaters in Moscow. But UIP wanted to earn hard currency, not rubles, so they decided to show them at the Sovincenter where foreigners stayed. They lined up *Moonstruck, Fatal Attraction,* and *Gremlins,* but I was concerned.

I told the client, "If you're a businessman in Moscow, you're just here to do business and don't have time for movies. If you're a tourist, you've probably already seen the movie. And there aren't enough English-speaking foreigners living here to support such a business by themselves."

I hated to lose a client by advising them not to enter this market, but our credibility was important. UIP was convinced the project would work and went ahead. But after a very short time, they realized they couldn't make money in the Sovincenter, and they closed up. Perhaps with a convertible ruble, they will have another go at the neighborhood cinemas where their films will no doubt succeed.

Another early project was to research the processed meat market for a Spanish company, Campofrio, which sold refrigerated processed meats like Oscar Mayer in the United States.

Again the research indicated they could sell all they could make.

From Soviet enterprises, we were hired to do research for a big watch factory, Poljot, and the biggest perfume factory, Novaya Zarya. They all wanted to know where they could sell their products outside the Soviet Union for hard currency. They weren't easy assignments because most Soviet-made goods weren't that appealing.

At a meeting at Factory #1, we suggested that Italy might be a market for the Soviet army watches for some quick sales because the Italians love fads. "But you don't want to build a business only on a short-term item," we warned the watch people. "You need a good reason for someone to want Russian watches. They've got to be cheaper or better. Otherwise the Swiss, Americans, and Japanese pretty much have the watch market locked up."

They thanked me for the advice and invited Freddye and me for tea with their president. The last time I heard, they were starting to make quartz watches instead of the old windups. And they were looking into selling the watches in Third World countries.

Even the Soviet industrial goods—locomotive parts, turbines, and other power-generating equipment—weren't of the standards that made them competitive in most of the West. One producer of windmills for energy asked us to find them a market. We worked closely with our São Paulo office to develop mailing lists for Latin America, where industrial goods are needed. While the Latin American currencies weren't much better than rubles, those countries had an abundance of foodstuffs (bananas, coffee, etc.) that could be used in straight barter deals. This was the only immediate way around a worthless ruble.

People came to us with all kinds of hare-brained schemes. Promoters offered us sponsorship opportunities for everything from dogsled races to balloon races. We were approached to find sponsors for the side of the Soviet space station MIR (peace), a Soviet gymnastics team, and bicycling team.

"Mike, are you sure we're in the ad business?" I lamented on more than one occasion after a parade of hustlers left our offices. In the beginning, we couldn't afford not to listen to these various pitches. You can't separate the wheat from the chaff until you hear the deal.

"I just don't know how many more cowboys I can stand to see," I told him. "Cowboys" were what we called all these big talkers that came in to do deals. I suspect they were there long before I arrived, proving that even in the motherland of communism, you can't stamp out capitalism in every form.

As soon as I first arrived, I realized that all the taxi drivers were out for a buck on the side. They wanted to trade money; they knew where they could find you a restaurant; they could get you women, or Soviet watches, or icons and paintings. What they especially wanted in return were Western goods. VCRs were the most desired item.

Once we opened the office and looked like a proper business, the parade of propositioners never stopped. No one was quite sure what Young & Rubicam/Sovero did; they just knew we looked like an international business and had a nice office.

Vlasov was the worst offender in opening the door to anyone who knocked. He saw us as the window to the world and would bring in all kinds of characters. They'd sit in his "private" office with the door closed for hours, drinking good Western coffee. Frequently, his buddy Fedorov and sometimes Pashin would be included. Now keep in mind that we had an open office system and the walls only extended eight feet high, so no one's office was completely private. At about three in the afternoon he'd come to my office and Mike's. "Gary, Mike, I'd like you to meet my good friends. They have a *very* interesting deal. They want to meet you."

We'd ask about three questions and they'd have either the wrong answers or no answers and we knew there was no work involving communications. One time, he had people in that wanted to sell wood to the Romanians, who would craft it into furniture and sell it to the West, so that both parties would get hard currency. Absolutely unrelated to advertising and PR, but Vlasov couldn't resist tempting side deals. Another time it was converting military plants into consumer manufacturing plants, and another a plywood deal.

"Vladimir, there's no communications work, so there's no deal." Vlasov stormed out of the office. He was looking for that elusive big-money-for-no-work deal that would secure his retirement. To make money without working was his big objective. That was his idea of what the new capitalism could offer.

Finally, I said to Vlasov, "Look, ask them the questions I do before they settle down in your office. If they don't give you the right answers, kindly show them the door. We don't have that kind of time to waste."

He grumbled that he would. We even taught Elena, the receptionist, how to question these guys so she could screen them.

"Wouldn't it be fun to create a Domino's pizza commercial, showing pizza being delivered on a Soviet space station? And we could put an STP sticker on the side of the rocket." I was coming up with all kinds of crazy ideas once I met with the spacecraft people.

I could see it now: Millions of people focused on our clients' logos as the craft soared skyward. NPO Energia came to sell us the sponsorship rights to the Soviet space program.

"We aren't interested in buying the rights, but maybe we

can come up with a program that would be interesting to both of us," I told them.

"Do you have the authority to grant us the rights?" I asked while looking at a single sheet of paper with very few details. They had no brochure, no photos.

They assured us they were the authorized licensing agent. So I asked the Burson-Marsteller group in New York that specializes in developing such programs to come up with some ideas. When I sat down with the NPO Energia people again, the Burson-Marsteller people had developed a whole binder outlining programs involving toys, T-shirts, and all sorts of product categories.

They thanked us, took the book, and left. The next thing we knew, some group in Texas claimed to have exclusive rights to the space program. It turned out that three different groups came to us offering "exclusive" rights—and that's when we learned about multiple exclusive agreements!

We made some Burson-Marsteller people back in New York awful mad that they had spent their weekend on work that was in effect given away free. It sure taught us that we had to be more careful. I don't think the Soviets were intentionally dishonest. I think they just didn't know the ethics and protocol of business in the West. They don't have the courtesies and the tradition that a handshake is as good as a signed contract.

Whenever we could find even a tenuous product link, we presented opportunities to our clients. We mentioned the balloon race to Kodak because it was so visual, and the dogsled race to Du Pont because we thought the fiber division might be interested in outfitting the team in fabrics using their branded fibers.

We had to be careful. Once, we got J&J involved in a telethon that was raising funds for orphan children. In return for providing about $25,000 worth of product, J&J was invited to appear on the program to receive a certificate honoring its participation, and to display and explain the products it would soon be bringing to the Soviet Union. The program seemed a good opportunity to grease the joint venture procedure for J&J.

Roman had worked hard to get J&J scheduled as one of the last companies on the show so that it would appear in "prime time." Unfortunately, the producers lost control, so there was time only for J&J to get a tiny mention in passing. I was furious and apologized to my client.

"Don't worry." Dearstyne was more understanding than I. "I've been kicking around this place long enough to know this can happen. We'll just consider the $25,000 worth of product a donation to a good cause."

We tried to encourage Gannett to start an outdoor business in Moscow. It would be nice to have a Western company involved in developing outdoor sites. We got them together with the appropriate people, but when they asked if we could promise that our clients would be interested in buying the space, I had to admit I wasn't optimistic for the short term. That, coupled with the fact that the package deal included buying a primitive neon sign company that was virtually worthless, quashed their interest.

Developing a relationship with Gosteleradio, the state committee that controls all broadcasting, was an important objective for us. For one reason, we heard they were looking for a consultant, and we knew that could help shape the commercial broadcast industry for years to come. For another, we wanted to know the people that would be airing our clients' commercials to make sure they understood our needs.

Getting into the door was not easy—in more ways than one. "I really don't want to meet with you," was the way the director greeted me. "We don't have a very good relationship with or opinion of your partner, Sovero. I'm only seeing you out of courtesy to my friend Fedorov."

Our account director, Valery Fedorov, again worked some magic, using his connections to get me in. It was all downhill from there, despite difficult logistics. As a foreigner, the large, relatively modern Gosteleradio building was one that I was not allowed to enter unaccompanied. It had an impressive lobby and lots of security. Once inside, everyone, even an employee, is required to check their coat at a huge coat-check stand with slow-moving retirees, and all foreign visitors must have an escort.

Once, when we were at the Gosteleradio building with an escort, we couldn't find our escort at the end of our meeting. So I suggested that we just leave the same way we came in. "No!" The Soviets were shocked. "No way! You can't go out the door alone. You must be escorted out." We left alone. Nothing happened to us. As we walked through the halls, I noticed that almost every office had a TV tuned to CNN. (There was a satellite dish on the roof.) Later, I asked a Soviet TV announcer about this, and he said, "How do you think we find out what is going on in the world?" Score another one for Ted Turner.

The role of Soviet television, under strict government control, has been that of a propaganda tool ever since TV came to the Soviet Union. News and talk shows carried whatever messages the Communist Party wanted to convey under the guise of independent thought. The TV people needed to start from ground zero to establish a Western-style station offering interesting programming, attracting viewers and advertisers. It was clear when I mentioned "dayparts" and "research" and "audience measurement" that they didn't know what I was talking about. The first task they wanted to accomplish was to set up a rate card, a price schedule for selling time. They didn't like our recommendation because we told them they had to prove they were worthwhile before they could charge a lot of money. They eventually gave that assignment to one of our rivals, Saatchi & Saatchi in London. Personally, I felt Saatchi did Gosteleradio a disservice by telling them that they could charge high prices in hard currency for advertising because they're the biggest network in the world. The result was that the high rates scared off many potential customers Gosteleradio might have had if they reduced rates to an experimental entry level.

It was hard to keep our focus on advertising. "We're not a doer of deals," I was constantly reminding Vlasov. "We're not a matchmaker or an expediter. If we have to get involved to bring in some related communications business, maybe. Otherwise, say no."

But I wasn't good at following my own direction. Sometimes we were just an escort service. Western companies attending some sort of trade show or congress would come visit our office.

"You guys must have figured out the system. You have phones that work and know how to get around." So they'd ask us to make their appointments or get them transportation or set up meetings for them with the appropriate government officials, even use our conference room. Admittedly, it was hard to say no. And we did feel we were helping to create a future advertising and PR client.

Sometimes, we could charge for these one-time services. I even toyed with the idea of becoming the first agency ever to accept the American Express card for its services. Once an attorney who put together East-West deals woke me at 7:00 A.M. one Saturday.

"Gary, I desperately need your help. We're trying to get a contract finished by tonight, and I can't find any word-processing center. How much do you rent your Macintoshes for?"

I was taken aback. Our Macintoshes weren't rental equipment. It never occurred to me they could be considered a profit center.

"Well, I don't know. Forty dollars an hour?"

"Sounds good to me. When can we get started?"

"Give me half an hour."

I probably could have charged him $100 an hour. Then he needed some blank floppy disks. So we came up with another fee.

After that, I began thinking maybe we should set up a simple desktop publishing company at night to keep the computers working round the clock to make some hard currency. On further thought, I didn't want to worry about taking the necessary precautions for security; but if we got really desperate for money, it was certainly feasible.

We used every connection we had to drum up business. Sometimes people came to us with a proposition that promised to be quite beneficial for both of us. We met with the Pulitzer Prize-winning author of *The Russians,* Hedrick Smith, who was trying to raise money for a PBS special on the Soviet Union. He was looking for a sponsor for a mini-series. He wanted $1.5 million and I wanted to meet him to pick his brain on this vast complex country that he had studied and written about in depth and with such insight. Unfortunately, we couldn't find him a sponsor after several months of trying.

Mike and I had a standing joke. It seemed every other person who came in the door had a hotel deal. After all, this was a country that was going to need everything, and people would want a decent place to stay when they came in to do business. At one time or another every hotel chain you can imagine was rumored to be doing a deal in Moscow.

Dozens of times we heard ambitious young entrepreneurs tell us about the space they wanted to renovate into a 200-room four-star hotel. All they needed was a "little" investment from the West.

"Where are all these hotels?" Mike would say time and

time again. "This place ought to look like Houston. And Houston it isn't."

They all got bogged down because no one could answer questions like who owned the building that was being converted and how were the people in it going to be taken care of. A lot of lawyers made a lot of money, but not much was accomplished in the end.

Once, I ran into former President Nixon's chief of staff, H. R. Haldeman, who was representing the Radisson hotel chain. His project got farther than most with a site and the start of construction. But like the others, something happened and it was never finished while I was there.

Every time Mike and I would discuss pitches we'd heard, our discussion would end up with something like, "Sergei wanted us to represent him selling hockey pucks, and, oh yeah, he had a hotel deal." It gave us a good laugh.

Even some of the promotional opportunities that came our way were highly suspect. A company called Afro Arab Company asked us to do the publicity and gave us sole production rights for a Miss U.S.S.R. contest. It was planned to take place in just two weeks—doomed to fail, I thought, because there was no time to do it right.

We were presented endless opportunities to sponsor everything from ballerinas to orchestras to gymnasts to cyclists. The Soviets wanted to field amateur and professional bike teams in the Coors race in Colorado. They figured they could make it to New York if a sponsor would pay their expenses from then on.

"You guys have big clients. Why can't you come up with just a bit of money?" we were asked time and time again. They wanted a baseball coach to come to the Soviet Union and teach baseball since it appeared that baseball would become a regular Olympic sport.

One good idea presented to us was the development of a sporting complex in the Caucasus Mountains, a place to bring foreign sportsmen for hunting, fishing, skiing, camping. The place was rustic, but a good idea because it didn't require lots of capital, would bring in hard currency, and would attract the hard-core sportsmen. There are enough devoted skiers around who would come even without modern plumbing to be able to say they'd skied in the Caucasus. We brought in specialists from Burson-Marsteller to work with us. But once again the deal went sour when the people we were working with didn't have the authority to develop the complex.

Part of the problem was that these were opportunists who smelled a quick buck, as a result of a little bit of knowledge about what goes on in the West in terms of licensing and getting endorsements. Nobody was sure who is in charge with all the changes Gorbachev had instituted. There are a lot of people who can say no, but only a few who can sign a contract and say yes.

At the end of our first year in business, we had a situation I never expected: a ruble profit for work for Soviet clients, and a minor dollar loss on the official joint venture books. These numbers did not include all the additional expatriate costs covered separately by Y&R.

When I had a particularly bad day, I would think about what we were doing here. What the Soviets really wanted was the ability to make their own consumer goods, so they would not have to buy exclusive imported goods from America or Japan or Europe. There were times when I thought our greatest value would be in advising people *not* to invest in the Soviet Union until ... until when? Well, until the ruble is convertible.

6

FREDDYE

FREDDYE IS THE MOST REALISTIC MEMBER OF OUR FAMILY.

When I heard about the opening of the office in Moscow, I was ready to jump in with both feet.

Not Freddye. She didn't forget to ask some important questions. "Where will we live? Where will Heather and Greta go to school?"

She instantly recognized this wasn't just *any* assignment overseas—something I had not overlooked so much as just assumed would take care of itself. Freddye brought me back to reality, reminding me that we needed to look into personal and family arrangements.

However, my assignment to Moscow was settled even before we got all the answers to her important concerns. Freddye and I agreed that I would accept the position and go from there. Would I commute? From the States, or London? From somewhere else in Europe—maybe Helsinki? Would we live as a family in Moscow? We had never lived apart before, and I didn't want to start now. But it became clear that renting an apartment in Moscow wasn't going to be like finding a home in New York—it wasn't just a matter of pounding the pavement with real estate brokers. We decided that Freddye and our daughters would remain in Connecticut at least through the school year.

Living accommodations turned out to be one of the stickiest points of the joint venture, since the Soviets had promised to find us a place to live. Apartments in Moscow are in short supply for Soviets—and more so for foreigners. Western-style apartments are even rarer. Allocations are made by the government, and we didn't appear to be very high on anyone's priority list.

As the weeks turned into months, we got promises and more promises from our partners. "We'll have something when you're ready to bring your family." Each time I heard that promise, I'd get a bit more skeptical.

Meanwhile, at home we debated about where the best location would be from the standpoint of family life and lifestyle. Then that was more or less taken out of our hands when the Soviets themselves said they wanted me to live in Moscow. That view was shared by Alex Kroll, who felt that if I was not in Moscow every day, Y&R would lack credibility with both Soviet and Western clients. He was right.

"I can't disagree, Freddye. It is important that I live in the marketplace I'm trying to learn." Freddye understood. The months sped by. Each trip I hoped I could come back and say, "We have a beautiful apartment in a lovely building in a desirable part of town. I can't wait for you to see it!"

Getting an apartment was a matter of waiting for the Soviets to find something for us. So, until they gave me the word, I couldn't even come back to Freddye and say, "We have an apartment," much less describe it.

I was a nomad, living in one hotel on one trip and in another the next. I never knew more than a couple days in advance where I would be staying. I got used to it, but I never liked it. I knew I couldn't live like that indefinitely, and Freddye wanted to know where she was going to call home for the next few years.

After I had been commuting for a few months on my own, Freddye came over with me. She can express her first impressions far better than I can.

When we arrived at Kennedy Airport for our flight, there were noticeable signals that Moscow was a different destination than London or Paris or Frankfurt. Security is very tight in the departure area. We stood in a long line inching our way to a glass-enclosed area where the X-ray machine would examine our carry-on luggage. A slight but wiry young Hispanic, conscientiously guarding the double glass doors, kept the line from flooding past by extending his arms and legs across the opening. After he examined our tickets, we passed through and stood at the check-in counter. I felt a sharp elbow jabbing my back. As I turned to glare at my assailant, I saw a stocky, elderly Russian woman, bundled in several layers of sweaters, all topped with a short brown fake leather jacket. Around her neck and trailing down her back was a feathery wool scarf. My glare did nothing to discourage her from pressing against me. She was oblivious to everything except the hugs presumably from her family, who stood just beyond a maroon velvet rope. I mumbled something to Gary about her herding instinct.

"This flight is always filled with Russians returning from visits with their families here," he told me.

"Do they always push?"

"It's pretty typical," he assured me.

Meanwhile, the dozen or so family members were wailing and taking photographs. The youngest of the lot—wee toddlers—were shoved into the woman's arms. Was she their grandmother? Their aunt? I don't know. Then another combination of folks would be photographed, their faces pressed cheek to cheek. Another round of tears and hugs.

Through all of this, she maintained her pressure on my back. Lucky for her I'm sentimental. I cry at stirring music. I'm moved by the farewells in life. So my sympathies kept me from countering the pressure by shoving her back.

When I looked around, I observed that most of the Russians in the line adopted this same aggressive stance, making for a huddled mass pressing forward. I had heard about the long lines in Moscow—lines for shoes, lines for food, lines for everything. I was surprised at their technique in forming "lines."

Then there was the direct aggressive approach of the "important" Russian. This gentleman was accompanied by two other men, all swathed in well-tailored gray wool overcoats, who pushed roughly past us and forced their way to the front. There, they bullied their way through the door into the restricted area. I'd like to say I was outraged as they pushed past without so much as an "excuse me," but my feelings ran toward disgust. Their action offended my very American notion of priorities and equality. I wondered what would have happened if I had grabbed their arms and said, "Wait a minute, buddy! Who crowned you king for a day?" I could see my culture clashing with theirs even before I reached the door that would lead to Flight 30.

The Moscow airport, built for the 1980 Olympics that the U.S. boycotted, is spacious, modern, and well kept. I slumped in a chair waiting for some progress to be made on our luggage. Most had come through quickly, but one person traveling with us was missing a typewriter. I figured it was already well on its way to some black market. As I slouched down, through a haze of fatigue I watched the Russians trying to identify their luggage. All the suitcases tumbling off the carousel looked alike, all large plastic cases in one of three colors, light blue, brown, and black. All were the same brand and style. Maybe they didn't have a brand name. Shoppers probably had no choice and took whatever they were lucky enough to find.

Finally, we were on our way to our hotel in downtown Moscow. En route, I observed that the apartment buildings illustrated as much variety as the suitcases, rows of sterile boxes. Only as we approached the inner city did the buildings become interesting, with an occasional onion-topped church or intriguing government edifice. The Moscow River provided relief, snaking its way among the boxes, softening the rigid rectangular lines. Even so, the overall picture was of gray. The streets, the dirt, the windows, the sky. Even gray people, young and old alike.

Where variety occurs, it's startling. My second day in Moscow, I sat with my interpreter, my lifeline, awaiting an interview with the director of one of the so-called English schools, a place where English is taught as the second language. The room was about 18 by 10 feet with a ceiling of perhaps 12 feet. It was spartan. A large window dominated the wall at the far end of the room. On its ledge sat two telephones, an old-fashioned black rotary dial and a more modern beige rotary dial with a black handset. Three small chairs were lined against the left wall. Opposite them was a small, sharp silver handle, attached to a door that blended almost indistinguishably into the wall. To its right was a brown Formica closet.

Mikhail and I made small talk as we sat waiting. Suddenly, an elderly woman, all in black including a scarf tied under her chin, shuffled into the room and over to the silver door handle. She grasped and jiggled it, but nothing happened. Muttering, she turned and without a glance at us left. Mikhail and I looked at each other and shrugged.

We had just settled back when a teenage boy in school uniform, blue blazer, tie, and gray slacks, strolled across the room and tried his luck with the silver handle. He turned and said something to us in Russian; Mikhail nodded and smiled but did not answer. The boy left also. We obviously weren't the only ones trying to see the director.

Then a middle-aged woman scurried across the floor, also trying the handle. She bustled out as fast as she entered. Next, I wouldn't have been surprised to see the White Rabbit muttering, "I'm late, I'm late," as he pulled his pocketwatch from his vest and tried the silver handle. I was about to comment on all the activity when one of the phones jangled loudly. Mikhail and I both sat staring at its incessant ringing. When it finally stopped, I looked up to see a beautifully dressed young mother coming into the room. She was perhaps 5 feet 8 inches, with short blond hair, and could have been a model in any Western country. As she leaned down, the longer hair strands in front fell across her profile and she flicked them back with a toss of her head.

She was dressed like no other Russian I had seen, in a beautifully tailored caramel-colored suede jacket and beige wool plaid skirt. Matching suede boots disappeared under her skirt. She carried a large brown leather bag that held a tennis racquet.

She seemed as much out of place as—well—even more so than I. She too tried the door handle, spoke to Mikhail, smiled, seemed to thank him, and taking her daughter by the hand, left.

Before I had a chance to ask Mikhail what was going on, he said, "She seems to be on the same mission as you are."

I was so in awe, I could only say, "She's so striking!"

"Striking?"

"Yes, beautiful and so well dressed."

The moment the words were out of my mouth, I almost bit my tongue. How could I be so tactless. How rude of me. I was embarrassed. Mikhail just smiled at me.

What contradictions in this mysterious land.

The next day as I walked from one appointment to another, I found myself enjoying the goings-on in a neighborhood park. Two teenage girls linked arm in arm giggled and whispered, probably about the same sorts of things that all teenage girls giggle and whisper about— their friends, their enemies, life's slings and arrows. They wore their hair like most of the girls their age, long and braided in a single fat plait down their backs, a much tidier and more attractive style than the wild, multi-layered frizzy hairdos of American teens.

Children played tag or sat with their toys. Boys raced around and followed their leader into mock battle. Some wallowed in the mud, as filthy as little boys anywhere. Mothers relaxed on benches gossiping, rocking their babies in carriages. Unaware of being watched by a foreigner, these women were like women anywhere, affectionate, having let down that impenetrable guard that I'd seen whenever Gary and I met Russians officially.

The notion of choice came up again when I accompanied Gary on a business meeting. The discussion was about finding out which of several meat products would appeal to the Russian palate. One Soviet at the meeting laughed. "Why would anyone care what 'the people' want? You buy what's available." He wasn't joking.

On my last day in Moscow, I ventured off to appointments in a limo with a driver provided by Y&R's Soviet partners. The idea of a limo in this environment of scarcity was uncomfortable. Even more awkward was the custom of sitting in the front seat beside the driver, who spoke no English, as we roared through the fast lane reserved for VIPs, ambulances, and government vehicles.

At the airport as I was on my way home, I couldn't help but compare the young soldier manning the passport control booth with the young American marine I had encountered earlier that week at the U.S. Embassy checkpoint. Both were young, fresh-faced, with that detached "long away from home" look of soldiers the world over. Had they switched uniforms, you couldn't have told them apart.

I flew home exhausted and confused, hopeful that I could adjust to life in a land that both beckoned and rebuffed at the same time.

I had such a feeling of emptiness that night after Freddye left. I wondered what she was thinking as she flew home. Or was *this* home? We were both nomads.

To join me, Freddye would once again have to put aside her own ambitions to accommodate mine. She was finishing up a degree in creative writing at a college in Connecticut and wanted to start her writing career.

Moscow didn't seem the ideal spot to achieve her goals. She has supported my career decisions ever since we were married in 1966. My work has taken us to live in Japan and Belgium and France. We've both enjoyed our lives as expats, and our two daughters have adapted very well to being outside the United States.

Our elder daughter, Heather, was already in college, so she had left home physically even though she was in touch almost daily by phone. Our younger daughter, Greta, was completing her sophomore year in high school and was not anxious to transfer to a new school.

Once Moscow beckoned, we began to explore the possibility of her attending school there. I had heard there was a decent international high school in Moscow, but then I discovered that it only went through tenth grade. If Greta were to come with us, she'd have to go to a local Soviet school, and since she knew no Russian, she'd probably lose a year. She wasn't prepared for that, so we spent months drying tears as we visited boarding schools in Europe and the States.

It was a sad time for me, and it dampened some of my excitement over my new job. I was emptying the nest early. Freddye herself was upset because Greta was so upset. "Perhaps the assignment will take too great a toll on my family," I thought, "or maybe I'm being too selfish." I had lots of doubts and second thoughts. But I pushed myself to go forward and find a way to make it work for all of us.

The search for the right school took us to Sweden, Austria, and England. If we hadn't been so tense and somewhat guilty about shipping Greta off, these trips to find a school could have been pleasant excursions. Greta and I drove through the beautiful landscape of southern Germany. It's even more charming than the illustrations on picture postcards — fairytale castles and picturesque villages in a land of gently rolling hills and deep blue lakes.

We took a day to be tourists. Ate delicious crispy Wienerschnitzel until we didn't want to *see* any more. Treated our-selves to a luxurious hotel.

"This school is too small," Greta decided after visiting one place with a fine reputation in Salzburg. There were only about one hundred students, but I liked it very much. We moved on. The London school also looked just like you read about: An old Tudor house, with beautifully manicured lawns; riding stables; rosy-cheeked girls in blue uniforms. The director was pleasant, witty, and helpful. But Greta wasn't impressed. The girls there told her, "Go someplace else. Anywhere else." Catty, giggly teens. And she followed their advice. "I want more choices," she told us.

So, we went back to Connecticut and drew up a list of schools in the States.

Throughout all of this, Y&R was understanding. They were supportive, but wanted me to take care of the personal arrangements on my own. "Take your time working it out," they told me. Peter Georgescu, president of Y&R Advertising in New York, was helpful in suggesting an education coun-selor who gave us some good advice.

It continued to be a difficult time. Freddye and I argued frequently. At last, Greta found a school that she didn't dis-like — in Richmond. Still, she was having a hard time thinking about breaking away. More tears. We decided not to think about next year's schooling for a while.

By summer, our plans were set. Greta would go to St. Catherine's in Richmond, and Heather would be at Goucher College in Maryland. Our Soviet partners found an apart-ment for us in the Mezh.

We began packing up our clothes and personal belongings. We found a housesitter. In early August, Freddye and I boarded the plane to start setting up the Moscow apartment. It had been an unbelievable ten months of uncertainty. On the plane, first class was filled with music executives and PR people on their way to a big Moscow rock festival. (I had enough Pan Am frequent-flyer miles to get upgraded from business class regularly.) In the next few days the Soviets would get their first taste of a major international rock concert. It was an exciting time for us, too. The girls would follow in a few days to have a look at our new home. All seven of our bags arrived intact. But we forgot one important item: our shower pole.

The apartment looked fresh and clean. It was small, only two rooms and a kitchen, a challenge to Freddye's decorating abilities. It would be a test of how well we four get along when the girls arrived, but it was all ours — finally.

Four days later, I was sleeping late (for me). I was sleeping better now than I had in months. Still, I woke up hours before Freddye, and I was trying to be quiet. It was our twenty-third anniversary. This place was beginning to feel like home with Freddye here. I would miss the girls, but we'd see them in the summers and on holidays in between. I looked forward to their visit with us these next few days. . . .

They have come and gone. The four days they spent with us were just long enough, especially in a one-bedroom apartment. Freddye kept them busy, and I think they enjoyed their trip, even though they found Moscow pretty grim. The highlight clearly was the rock concert: Bon Jovi. Heavy metal is not my favorite, but I enjoyed being with the girls. Freddye and I had gone the previous day and she declined a second visit, so I invited the "other" Volodya — our temporary driver — who called himself my brother in unpopular wars. He was very protective of us in the huge crowd and seemed to enjoy the music.

Throughout their stay, in the back of all of our minds were those few days when we would gather for the last time in Westport before we all took off in different directions. Then, before we knew it, it was time to head for . . . do I still call Westport home? We had lots to do there, packing, getting the girls off to school. Although we were busy, it was an awful time. Greta cried the whole last weekend we were together. She cried when we said goodbye after driving her to Richmond. In the car on the way back, Freddye alternated between tears, anger, and silence.

If I had known how hard this part of our life was going to be, I might not have worked so hard for the job. Everyone was unhappy.

Freddye and I finished packing, completed shopping, reminded ourselves not to forget the shower pole. It was with seesawing emotions that we said goodbye to Westport for who knew how long.

Once settled in Moscow, I could plunge into my work, but Freddye had nothing to keep her mind from wandering back to where part of her heart was, wondering what Heather and Greta were doing. Were they managing? She started Russian lessons, and worked hard at it. She shopped creatively. I was amazed at how she could make fabulous dinners with limited cooking facilities and meager ingredients. But that was not enough to keep her fulfilled. I wanted so much for this adventure to be as exciting for her as it was for me. So many wives give up after just a few weeks.

Only I know Freddye's pain. She's put on a good face for our stream of visitors, clients, and Y&R executives. She's been terrific in entertaining the wives. Now, weeks later, we're settling in. She's been hired as a substitute teacher at the International Elementary School, teaching the computer to young children. It's a long way out on Leninsky

Prospekt; she takes the Metro in the morning before day-light and returns at the end of the day. She's gained confi-dence in her ability to cope and navigate this imposing city.

She's still anxious about riding in Russian elevators, except in the Sovincenter and at the embassy. I can't blame her. They're creaky, and are prone to lurching and stopping sud-denly for no reason, only to grind upward again.

We couldn't help wondering whether we could have found better apartments on our own. To satisfy that curiosity, we set out to look at some apartments that Vlasov insisted were too far out and weren't worth looking at. We didn't believe him and felt he was trying to keep us from seeing them. So we sneakily went to check them out.

They *were* far out, beyond the last Metro stop. We walked for quite a while before finally finding them. Seeing them in the last stages of construction, we waded through mud that oozed up to the tops of our shoes and had to climb some metal grid lathing that Volodya found to gain access to the building through a window. I remember standing in the street wiping the thick brown goo off our shoes before we got back into the car. Now when I think back about that apartment-hunting expedition, I just laugh at how ludicrous it was. It turned out Vlasov was right. Those apartments were not for us. We appreciated our small, cozy home even more.

Then, suddenly, Freddye became almost as busy as I was. She was appointed publisher/editor of our agency's bi-weekly business press review. I asked her to collect clippings from publications that would be of interest to our clients and prospects in Moscow. She scoured newspapers and business publications, extracting stories about Soviet business dealings.

"Freddye, you're doing a terrific job. This is a great service. Keep it coming," several expats told her after the first issue.

"You know, I think we could even sell subscriptions," I said.

Since we were using the review as a new business tool, and to establish Y&R/Sovero as an information source, providing names of businesses coming in, we decided to continue sending it out for free.

Our biggest problem was lack of paper. We were careful to use both sides of paper in the copy machine. The Soviets had taught us to save all scraps. "Natalie, why are you going through that trash?" I asked one day not long after we moved into the office. "Someone has thrown out paperclips," she said. "I'm looking for them." From then on we were more careful, and we learned to use pencils down to the half-inch.

Freddye also began teaching the staff how to use the Mac. She became a role model for Natalie, who asked her advice on all kinds of women's issues and how women in business conduct themselves. All the women in the office wanted Freddye to tell them about life in the West. To them she seemed more approachable than Mike or me.

She finally made the emotional break with the kids. She accepted that Greta and Heather were happy wrapped up in their own lives. Greta was learning to be resourceful, especially after running out of money and being unable to reach us by phone for several days. She realized that other members of the family – her grandparents, aunts and uncles – are there for more than just vacation visits.

So, Freddye was now tackling living here with a vengeance. We were reminded daily of the sheer difficulty of surviving. When we went to the hard currency store each Saturday to do our food shopping, it was an emotional drain. As we carried our plastic bags filled with groceries out to the car, we passed through a throng of Russians begging to *buy* food from us with rubles.

Official signing: Gary Burandt (*left*) reviews legal documents with Yuri Deomidov, director general of Vneshtorgreklama (*center*), and Vladimir Vlasov, the senior Soviet in the joint venture. *Photo courtesy of Mike Adams*

The Soviet method of apartment hunting: Freddye Burandt (*right*) surveys the territory with friends.
Photo courtesy of Gary Burandt

Michael Adams wonders if the office, a storefront within sight of the American Embassy, will ever be ready. This space later had to be abandoned because the building's top floor was believed to be used for surveillance purposes.
Photo courtesy of Gary Burandt

The disappearance of a necessity? Michael Adams came back to this bathroom at the Intourist Hotel late one night after a long workday.
Photo courtesy of Mike Adams

A time to celebrate: The Y&R/Sovero staffers show off their newly acquired business cards, putting on their most pleasant expressions for the camera. *From left*: Vladimir Vlasov, Yuri Pashin, Roman Diukarev, Valery Fedorov, Mikhail Stroykov and Gary Burandt. *Photo courtesy of John Miller*

Gary Burandt (*left*) and Vladimir Vlasov during a rare moment of levity. *Photo courtesy of John Miller*

Luc De Leersnyder, head of Young & Rubicam's Brussels office, makes a presentation to execs from Gosteleradio on how to commercialize television.
Photo courtesy of Gary Burandt

Some of the first advertising for foreign brands seen in downtown Moscow near Red Square, automated outdoor posters for Pepsi and Daewoo.
Photo courtesy of Gary Burandt

Natasha Ovchinnikova became the first research director of an ad agency in Moscow when she left the Institute for Sociology Research to join Y&R/Sovero. *Photo courtesy of Gary Burandt*

Yuri Deomidov (*left*), General Manager of Sovero, and Mitch Kurz of Young & Rubicam during the early days of joint-venture negotiations. *Photo courtesy of Gary Burandt*

A contrast in styles between the two senior executives in the joint venture: Gary Burandt signals the victorious completion of furnishing the office (*above*), while Vladimir Vlasov's formal demeanor is aptly depicted in this passport photo. *Photo of Gary Burandt courtesy of Ellen Goldman*

Roman Diukarev proudly displays the air line ticket for his first trip to the U.S.
Photo courtesy of Gary Burandt

Hard-working Natalie Belova (*above right*) quickly rose from receptionist to account executive and master of the Macintosh.
Photo courtesy of Gary Burandt

Volodya, the office driver, relaxes in the Y&R/Sovero reception area.
Photo courtesy of Ellen Goldman

Michael Adams hard at work . . . as usual.
Photo courtesy of Gary Burandt

Partners and pioneers: Michael Adams (*left*) and Gary Burandt share a casual moment after putting together the office furniture.
Photo courtesy of Ellen Goldman

The staff prepares for an early morning training session in the conference room led by Luc De Leersnyder (*center*), head of Young & Rubicam's Brussels office. *From left*: Yuri Birasov, Roman Diukarev, Valery Fedorov, De Leersnyder, Yuri Pashin, Natalie Belova, Elena Golubera. *Photo courtesy of Gary Burandt*

One day, a woman stuffed a handful of rubles into Freddye's hand. "I have money. I have money, but I'm not allowed in," she said in Russian.

I felt awful, but by law I could not sell her our food. I told myself that it was their system, and one that I alone could not change by selling her food. But that didn't make me feel a lot better for the woman begging for something to eat.

Driving a car was another challenge. But Freddye's feisty spirit gave her the courage to do what she had to do to gain the independence that driving provided.

The first time she took the car out of the garage the security guard stared in amazement. Not many foreigners ventured out on their own, especially women. He walked over to watch her as if to say, "I want to see this miracle."

Once she was driving in downtown Moscow with Mike's wife, Barb. "I was making a right turn when I saw a policeman come running over shaking his stick at me," she told me later. "I rolled down the window and tried hard to understand what he was saying. Even though he spoke slowly and I concentrated on every word, I just couldn't tell what I'd done wrong."

Some of the traffic rules are very confusing. In some intersections, you cannot turn right on green but must wait for an arrow indicating a right turn is permitted. Freddye was at one of those intersections and finally realized what she had done. But by then the mili man had given up trying to make her understand. "After several minutes, he just threw up his hands and kindly waved me on."

"Well, I wonder how many times you'll get away with that," Barb said, laughing.

After several months, Freddye spoke enough Russian to be able to answer Volodya's questions. "How long have you been driving?" He wanted to know.

"Over twenty-five years," she told him.

"In the United States?"

"Japan and France and Belgium and all over the world."

"Even in New York City?"

"Yes, even in New York City," she admitted.

"There are lots of cars there, huh?"

"Yes, lots of cars."

He still frowned upon Freddye's driving, especially in "his" cars. That was understandable since the percentage of women drivers in the Soviet Union is very, very low.

The weeks Freddye and I were together in Moscow turned into months. Eventually both of us settled into satisfying routines.

7

BUSINESS AS USUAL

"HEY, MIKE, I'VE DISCOVERED ONE THING THAT'S NO DIFFERENT about working here than back home."

"What's that?" Mike grumbled. He, like the rest of us, was operating in overdrive. Tired and with a short fuse, he wasn't up to casual conversation.

It was October, and we were still exhausted from getting the office ready for the official opening while helping clients with *the* first major U.S. trade show ever at the same time.

"Important deadlines always seem to fall at the same time no matter where you are." I tried to nudge Mike into a cheerier mood.

"Uh-huh."

I looked with disgust at my desk piled high with stacks of papers that came in our twice-weekly Express Mail package from New York. The time pressures we were under to get clients ready for the show reminded me of a project I worked on several years earlier when the Sperry and Burroughs companies combined.

It was 1986. I was just back in New York from working two years in Paris. Young & Rubicam was one of several major worldwide agencies pitching to get the assignment to produce a communications campaign introducing the new computer company and the new name around the world. I was asked to get involved because I had some computer experience and an international background.

Our proposal won. "We'll be announcing the new company in two months. You have sixty days to prepare the work," our new client told us.

This kind of project often takes more than twice that long. We knew it would be a challenge, but I had no doubt that we were up to it. We could call on Y&R's professional worldwide network at a moment's notice, and we had a wealth of resources at our fingertips.

"I know this complicates matters, but we won't be able to provide you with the name of the new company until just a few days before we want the advertising to appear," the client said.

The company, in fact, didn't have a name at that point. Management was conducting a contest among employees to select a new name, and they were sifting through thousands of entries. Then, after the name was chosen, a search had to be done around the world to make sure it was legally clear.

Meanwhile, we were working on the advertising. We presented the headline and illustrations and the theme line because we didn't know enough yet to write the body copy. The client approved the concept and theme—"The power of 2"—so we started writing copy and taking photos.

An even bigger disadvantage than not knowing the company's name was not knowing where the company was headed, its mission, or its future. Management was worrying about hundreds of things that go with a merger of this magnitude, and while the advertising was important to them, it was only one of many problems they were working on simultaneously: Which jobs were going to remain? Who was going to get them? Who would be asked to leave?

So, we were left to come up with a safe, all-encompassing, but powerful message without the benefit of much information about our new client. "The power of 2" was a good line and one that suggested that the whole was better than the sum of its parts.

It was on this project that I first met Jeanette Lerman, who was head of corporate communications at Burroughs and would get that job at the new company. She had dozens of things to take care of, but was very accessible and would fly to New York when we needed to meet, or make time for us in her busy schedule in Detroit. Just finding out who were the right people to approve the copy was a job because the legal departments were in turmoil. But somehow we got all that done for the four ads and TV commercial that would run on the same day in forty-six countries in twelve languages.

Then we sent the copy out to our offices around the world to translate into local languages. Where the name of the new company was used, we left a blank.

One additional problem we faced was that Young & Rubicam was the new agency for a new company and had not worked for either Sperry or Burroughs before. We were bringing copy to a new client in countries where often we knew more about their new company than they did. And in each locale they were going through the same merger mania as in the United States. So, advertising copy was not of the highest priority to them. It was a stressful time for everyone, and Y&R was not necessarily their choice of agency. In some instances, they were resentful that they had to break up old ties with previous favorite agencies that in some cases had been established years earlier. It wasn't the best of circumstances, but we finally got everything completed — except for inserting the new name.

Just days before the ads were to appear, Jeanette said, "All I can tell you right now is the name has six letters, and," she added in case it was helpful in our graphics planning, "there's a tall letter in the middle."

The staff — there were about thirty of us — laughed when I passed along that bit of information. We sent out mechanicals of the ads to all countries, but left a six-space blank where the new name would go. At the eleventh hour, our client told us the name was Unisys. We faxed the name — with the tall letter "i" in the middle — to our offices around the world; they had the type set locally and dropped it into the ads. The day after Michael Blumenthal, chairman of the company, announced the new name, the ads were in the press.

We were proud of the job we'd done. We'd put together this herculean effort in just sixty days, and it all worked. We met the deadline and there were no security leaks. For our team, which had worked nonstop for sixty days, we made up T-shirts that said: I SURVIVED THE UNISYS CRISIS.

It was a gigantic task that worked because we were all pros. With a common language, we could apply standard techniques; we had machines that worked — computers, faxes, telexes, copiers — and use them we did, virtually nonstop. In a nutshell, it was Y&R at its best.

I chuckled as I thought back to those tense days and endless nights because, aside from the time pressure, it was the antithesis of working here in Moscow.

When Mike saw me grinning, he perked up. "Sorry I'm in such a foul mood," he apologized. "What's so funny?"

"I was just thinking about another tough assignment I worked on a few years ago," and I told him my experience on Unisys.

"What a contrast," I went on. "Here there are no professionals, no business machines that work; no tradition of 'Okay, this is an important mission, we have to serve the client,' and no attitude that you do whatever you have to do for the client."

"So which is harder?" Mike asked.

"I can't say. Just different. And, of course, our work here is ongoing. Unisys was intense, but we knew when the endpoint was. When I came here, I didn't know what to expect, but I guess I did assume that someone at Sovero would know about the basics of the advertising business."

"The Soviets think advertising and marketing are synonymous with selling. I guess that's why they feel more at home at trade shows than with media advertising. They think that's the best way to sell," Mike pointed out.

"I see that now, but what's so hard about understanding that you do the research; develop a strategy; from the strategy you come up with a powerful selling idea; you execute the idea; put it in the media; and you measure the results? It's a pretty simple business."

"You're right," Mike agreed. "But it's been seventy years since there's been any incentive for people to take initiative on their own. So, nothing is simple. It's no wonder you can't find the right people, the right tools, or even the right thinking. The Soviets aren't the wrong people, but they don't have the experience, the machine aids, or the service-oriented attitude."

"Yeah, and without those qualities our Unisys project would never have turned out the great success that it was, either."

"We'll have the same great success with this trade show. Our staff will come through. They're learning fast. They're working hard. They're showing pride in their work." Mike's usual optimism and enthusiasm were returning.

This trade show put us under tremendous pressure because we had so many clients that needed their work prepared at the same time. One of them, Colgate, decided only two months before the opening to be an exhibitor at this important show. For months, they hesitated to enter.

"Frankly, I don't think the exhibition is worth the effort and the expense," one representative insisted.

"You know how important trade shows are here." I urged Colgate to participate.

"Yes, but it will be so long before we'll need to advertise, and the logistics of all this will be so time-consuming and virtually thankless." The Colgate people were not convinced.

"I know that, but I think it's important that you be represented. You want the Soviets to recognize the Colgate name as the most important marketer of toothpaste and other personal care products in the world."

Trade shows serve as an important advertising and promotional medium in countries like the Soviet Union, where there's no media available for advertising. The shows provide information about products that can't be obtained elsewhere. They also give the Soviet Union the opportunity to rent out space to foreigners for hard currency, and bring in people with hard currency to spend on hotels, restaurants, souvenirs, and so on.

The debate with Colgate continued until they heard that Procter & Gamble was gearing up to enter the Soviet Union with toothpaste. Demand for toothpaste will outstrip supply for years. But there's nothing like a good old-fashioned rivalry to spur companies to action.

By the time plans for the show were in full gear, we were working also with J&J and General Electric on their exhibits and promotions.

As opening day drew near, Sheremetievo Airport made an astonishing announcement: "We're closing for any additional air freight." All the stands and product exhibits and samples had clogged the facilities. The Soviet way of dealing with the overload was to shut down. Rather than add more staff and work overtime to move the goods out of the airport into the exhibit hall, the airport management simply decided: "No more."

The exhibitors' goods sat in other airports around the world while companies yelled at the Soviet government. "If you want us to bring in our goods and our money, you must accommodate us!" It was at this point that we learned that our office phones were sitting in Germany waiting for the airport to open. Mike, good sport and conscientious manager that he is, suffered the three-and-a-half-hour trip to Düsseldorf and another three-and-a-half-hour-trip back the same day stuffed into a coach seat on Aeroflot so that he could hand-carry in our phone equipment to have it in time for the official office opening. That way, the equipment could bypass the air freight logjam.

Some companies arranged to bring their goods in by flying them to Helsinki and having them make the two-day drive by truck. Other goods came in by ship to a port on the Black Sea.

Those of us who were becoming familiar with the Soviet style weren't surprised. "It's a mess," I allowed, "but not surprising." One way or another our clients were resourceful enough to get their goods in. Volodya was a big help, working his magic at the airport for our clients.

Opening day dawned bright, taking the edge off the long

night's chill, a hint at the long, hard winter to come in this capital city. I shivered as I walked the few blocks from our office to the exhibition hall. Once the exhibition center loomed in sight, perched impressively on the bank of the Moscow River, I couldn't believe what I saw: A seemingly endless line of Muscovites snaked around corners. People willing to withstand a biting wind huddled together for a chance to glimpse much-desired Western goods that might be theirs if only Western companies could find a way to make business feasible in this vast commercial wasteland. Stamping their feet to stay warm, they must have been there since before daybreak. Another enterprising American was selling them Nathan's Famous hot dogs from a specially equipped truck if they had hard currency. Somehow, he had managed to get the franks shipped in without spoiling.

I was early and had no trouble getting into the exhibitors' entrance. Inside, everyone was bustling to put the finishing touches on their booths, making sure products were aligned and nicely presented. I checked out our clients' booths to see if they were ready for the hordes that would push through the doors and if there was anything more we could do for them before the opening. Another important task was to find out the path Gorbachev would take when he came to cut the ribbon to inaugurate the show. We needed to position key client execs in such a way as to give them a chance to shake the president's hand as he passed through the aisles.

We remembered the broad press coverage that Don Kendall of Pepsi-Cola got back in 1959 when he thrust a bottle of Pepsi into Khrushchev's hand. Photographs witnessing Pepsi diplomacy appeared in hundreds of newspapers across the United States and around the world. It took fifteen years before Pepsi actually began to be produced in the Soviet

Union, but the result was a twenty-year headstart for Pepsi over Coke.

I was especially hopeful that Bill Dearstyne of J&J would get a chance to meet with Gorbachev. When the Soviet leader made his way down the aisle where both J&J and Colgate had booths, he was surrounded by bodyguards and a mass of media. I saw Dearstyne directly in his path. "You're on, Bill," I thought.

From across the aisle I could see Gorbachev coming closer and my 6-foot, 3-inch friend towering over a short but commanding figure. I saw them grasp hands. Then they chatted for a minute or so. Bill was looking down and gesturing to the Band-Aids, baby products, and assortment of other Johnson products in the big display. I felt a great deal of satisfaction when Gorbachev looked up at Bill, smiled, and nodded as the interpreter translated Bill's remarks. They shook hands again, then he was gone toward the Colgate booth.

We had the Colgate representative also prepped for a "photo op" with a giant tube of Colgate "Big Red" toothpaste, the biggest we had. It worked. He shook Gorbachev's hand and handed him the toothpaste. As the Big Red box changed hands, a hundred camera shutters clicked as one. One of the photos would be in the Colgate boardroom in just a few days.

I was especially proud of the Colgate booth. We had designed it to be bright and colorful, displaying row upon row of Colgate toothpaste, toothbrushes, and other Colgate products: soaps, detergents, cosmetics, laundry and dishwashing aids.

Young Soviet women dressed in bright red skirts and white blouses with red Colgate sashes staffed the booth. They were from the advanced English program of the Institute of Foreign Languages in Moscow, so they could speak to us and the clients, as well as to the visitors to the exhibit. Their job was to look charming, answer any questions about the products, and pass out samples.

Colgate's exhibit drew a big crowd, not only because it was attractive and full of wondrous new products, but also because we were passing out free samples of Colgate toothpaste. Our neighbors on either side were not so pleased, even though they benefited from the increase in traffic. The line that formed to wait for samples blocked the nearby booths. We tried all sorts of queuing patterns to make everyone happy—and the other exhibitors tried to be good sports.

We also found we had to have an additional staffer to act as a runner to a back room to replace the tubes of toothpaste handed out on a continuous basis. Since we didn't have much storage in the booth itself, the runner retraced steps more than a dozen times a day, hauling out cases of toothpaste. We watched Muscovites gratefully take a tube, stuff it into one pocket, then return to the end of the line for another hour's wait for the tiny sample tube.

"Don't forget we're experts at waiting in line," Fedorov reminded me when he saw how puzzled I was.

The same thing happened at booths for Coke and Pepsi because they were dispensing free soft drinks, and at Archer Daniels Midland, handling out free soybean burgers. If you've never had a real burger, a soyburger tastes great. In fact, after you've been in Moscow for a few months, even if you're a burger aficionado, a soyburger tastes great.

Gorbachev moved on to the G.E. booth, then to the IBM booth, where he spent quite a long time playing with the PCs and talking to Burt Polishook, the manager in charge of Soviet operations. More handshakes, more photos—one of which, of Burt and the president, would make most of next day's papers around the world.

"Mike, I think we're going to make more on this show than on any other project of the year," I exclaimed.

The show went on for nearly a week. The lines grew longer each day as word spread about the free samples. Luckily, we estimated correctly and ended up with only about twenty extra cases of toothpaste, which we donated to a Moscow orphanage in Colgate's name.

Our assignment from Colgate did turn out to be the single biggest money-making project of the year for us. More important, it gave us some invaluable experience and positioned us as an expert in the logistics of exhibiting at a trade show in Moscow. As we helped our clients not only to prepare and translate materials but also to get goods delivered from the airport, warehoused, and moved into the exhibition hall, we learned the ins and outs of distribution and how to get things done despite the bureaucratic mess of a system.

Our clients rated the show a big success, too. Colgate gave away more than 70,000 tubes of toothpaste. Almost all the clients had photos of execs standing near Gorbachev either shaking his hand or giving him samples. This was a photo they could blow up, frame, proudly display in their Moscow offices, and send home to corporate headquarters.

The money we made from the show helped justify our existence. But the satisfaction that we had in meeting the challenge of serving our clients the Y&R way in the Soviet Union was the biggest reward of all.

"We did it, Mike. We're here to stay." All the hard work had finally paid off.

8

MY NEMESIS

Mike walked into Vladimir Vlasov's Vneshtorgreklama office and dumped a pile of papers on his desk.

"Good morning."

Vlasov peered at Mike with a look that was even sterner than usual. Without any word of greeting, he began shouting. "You see this." He picked up his phone receiver and started shaking it at Mike. "Listen to it!"

Mike listened.

"What do you hear?"

"Nothing," Mike said. The phone was dead.

"That's because you called me on it. You call me on this phone the first time, it will be down three or four days. You call me again, it will be out two weeks. You call me a third time, three months. After that, no more phone."

"Is that true?" Mike didn't know whether to believe him.

Vlasov just glared.

"I'm sorry, Vlasov. I can't do anything about that. That's

not tolerable. You work for a joint venture and you have to be accessible to your foreign partners. Look, if this phone business is true, go to Deomidov, and if that doesn't work, go to Golanov and Malkevich, and on up the line."

Vlasov threw his hands up in the air. The message: The Americans just don't understand.

Since our own offices still weren't ready, Mike had been working across the desk in Vlasov's closet of an office for some weeks. A few days before the phone blowup he heard Vlasov give someone the number of his direct line. Until then, he and I were using the "protocol" line into Vneshtorgreklama to reach Vlasov. That meant the front desk would call Vlasov down to a special phone on a different floor. It wasn't very convenient. We didn't realize he could be reached by a direct line.

Mike had used the direct number the day before to tell Vlasov he was held up and couldn't make an appointment. There was no sign of any concern in Vlasov's voice then, and no indication of his rage until Mike went into work the next day.

Whether Vlasov's phone was "out of order" because a foreigner (Mike) called on it was of little concern to us. We weren't willing to put up with any such nonsense when we were working hard in good faith to set up a viable business with Soviet partners.

Vlasov was an old party man and just couldn't break out of that mold. I often wondered why he was picked to be my counterpart, replacing "Vladimir the Slick" in the joint venture. From our perspective, he wasn't the ideal leader for the Soviet side. But then, no one asked us. And it's possible he was selected for that old party mentality: To keep us in line.

By Soviet standards, Vlasov was considered quite competent. A man in his sixties, he was one of three or four senior lieutenants reporting to Deomidov, the director at Vneshtorg-reklama. He spent most of his life in foreign trade and foreign service rather than communication. I'm not sure how he ended up at Vneshtorgreklama — perhaps because of his language skills.

His diplomatic jobs had taken him on stints in Chad, Iceland, India, Belgium — and he could handle himself well with foreigners. Like many Soviets, his manner was formal although not offensive. A stout man of about 5 feet, 8 inches, he had a stiff walk and stiff countenance, gray hair and gray eyebrows. In fact, he was overall a gray kind of person, who blended well into the gray society and establishment in Moscow.

His foreign assignments meant he was well connected — or had been at one time — since the best job for a Soviet was outside the Soviet Union. A posting almost anywhere outside the country guaranteed a better lifestyle and more freedom.

Once when we were having publicity pictures taken, I asked Vlasov, "Why do Soviets always look so grim in photographs?"

"Smiling makes you look silly. We take things seriously here," he told me.

In a purely social situation, Vlasov could be quite charming. One evening soon after we signed the contract, Freddye was visiting, and we took Vlasov and his wife Trina out to dinner at 36 Kropotkinskaya, the first and the best cooperative restaurant.

Mrs. Vlasov didn't speak a word of English, and Vlasov served as the translator, but it was quite a pleasant evening. We all chatted proudly about our children — they had a son and daughter, both grown up — and we had in common the city of Brussels, where we all had lived at one time.

But the relative ease of that social evening didn't carry

back to the office or over into our business relationship. My dealings with Vlasov were one continual confrontation over just about everything.

Once, when I was bitching about not having any decent place for our families to live, he began telling me about the grass hut he had had to live in for twelve months in Chad—and without his family. "Well, that's the difference between our system and yours," I shot back at him. "We don't intend to live that way."

One of our longest-running disputes was over cars. "Gary, every Soviet in joint ventures gets a Volvo," he told me soon after our agreement was signed.

"That's not practical, Vladimir. Besides, most of our staff have access to cars anyway."

"A foreign car is one of the reasons people work in a joint venture," he said. "The staff deserves to be treated like other jv workers."

"Vlasov, you know our jv agreement calls for two office cars. And they won't be Volvos, they'll be Fords."

"Fords?" He was puzzled. "They're not represented in Moscow."

"Ford is a major Y&R client. That's how we do business."

I knew that Volvos were considered very prestigious in Moscow. I also knew that we wouldn't be buying them, and we wouldn't buy more than two cars. The plan was that the cars would be for office business during the week, and Mike and I would use them on the weekends.

Vlasov wouldn't give up. Every week we'd have the same argument. "You must go to the board of directors to get approval for more cars."

"Vlasov, I'm not going to do that. It's not a wise use of our precious hard currency."

The rigid Soviet system was ingrained in Vlasov. Totally

inflexible, he did everything by the book. One day as we were rushing around trying to get the office together, he asked me, "What's our per diem?"

"Nobody's taking a trip. We don't have to worry about that now." I was trying to get out of another battle with him.

"It's important."

"Are you planning a trip?" I asked him.

"Well, maybe. You never know when you have to travel abroad. But it's important anyway."

I didn't want to have this discussion now.

"We just don't work with a per diem," I told him. "When you travel on business, you stay in a good hotel. Not fancy, but comfortable and safe. You eat meals and take taxis and whatever it comes to, that's what we'll reimburse."

"Well, we don't have any hard currency. We'll have to take cash advances."

"That's fine," I told him. "That's the way it's done sometimes."

Discussion over. Then he would bring the issue up a few days later, and we would have virtually the same conversation. Finally, I figured maybe we could settle this matter once and for all, and we sat down to talk.

"We have to issue an order to the staff," Vlasov said flatly.

"What do you mean, 'issue an order'? Look, there's only eight of us. We'll just call everyone in and tell them."

"No, no. You have to have a written order."

I was baffled. What was the big deal? Several times I told him, "Executives are expected to use good judgment with the company's money, and they'll be reimbursed. Sometimes when you're traveling with a client, you don't have any choice of where to stay if a client wants a certain hotel."

"Well, how much is a hotel in New York City?" he asked.

"Y&R puts people up at the Hyatt, where we have a corporate rate. It's nice and close to the office at Fortieth and Madison. It's about one hundred and forty dollars a night."

"That's so expensive. What about food?"

"Oh, I don't know. Ten dollars for breakfast, fifteen for lunch, and twenty for dinner. Vladimir, I know that sounds expensive, but you pay what you have to pay. New York is an expensive city."

"Gary, do you know that Soviets get twenty-eight dollars a day for their expenses when they go to New York City?"

"Where do they stay for that?" I was amazed.

"There's a hotel over near Madison Square Garden where a lot of Soviets stay."

I couldn't imagine what kind of accommodations they were. Vlasov asked me if you could get a decent hotel room for one hundred dollars, and I told him it was probably possible.

"Okay, we'll make one hundred fifty the maximum per diem for hotel, food, taxis, everything. Nobody can go over that, and if they do, they'll get punished."

"Hold it, Vladimir. Punished? What are you going to do to them? Look, Mike and I aren't going to agree to a hundred and fifty dollars a day in New York, and I'm not going to make that a requirement for the staff."

"You're not showing good faith. It's the law of joint ventures."

I said I didn't think that was true, so Vlasov went off to find a written law about per diems.

It turned out that what Vlasov was getting at was not daily expenses at all. He was trying to find out how much money Soviets traveling abroad would have left over to buy Western goods. Typically, when Soviets travel outside the country "on business," they are given a daily living allowance in hard currency by the government since most don't have access to anything other than rubles. Any money left over is theirs. Scrimping on expenses allows them to buy coveted VCRs, shoes, clothes, food, and other "luxuries" unavailable in their own country. So they try to stay with friends when possible and have someone meet them at the airport or take the cheapest transportation.

It finally occurred to me what the issue was when Vlasov mentioned that Soviets always bring back souvenirs and gifts and that the allowance includes money for that purpose. Once I understood and addressed that directly, he never brought up the subject again.

"Gifts and souvenirs are personal expenses. The joint venture can't pay for them," I told him.

Officially, I was on record as taking the official position. Unofficially, frankly, I didn't care, and hoped they could squeeze as much private money as possible from the per diem. They got so little for their labors from their ruble salary. I decided to look the other way on per diem because I felt so badly about how these people had to live, and I said to myself that I'd consider the per diem an additional compensation to the meager salary set by the Soviets.

Although he fought for the per diem, he wouldn't give staffers some small gifts that were intended for them. Vlasov was a man of many contradictions. Every time a different side of him surfaced, I was surprised. One day he and Mike were working on a project together, and he got up to open the safe that was his pride and joy. Mike and I rarely used the safe because we didn't have anything that needed that kind of security. When Vlasov opened the door, Mike noticed that he had stashed away all the small gifts we had brought with us for the staff during the negotiations.

Vlasov didn't realize that Mike had seen the pile of gifts, but Pashin, who was working alongside them, did, and he seemed embarrassed that gifts supposed to have gone to the staffers hadn't been distributed. They weren't anything valuable — mostly corporate premiums with logos, pads of paper and pens, lighters, those kinds of things. But they would have been dear to the staffers they were meant for.

Later, Pashin told Mike that Vlasov's rationale for not distributing the items was that he didn't know if the joint venture was going to work, and if it didn't they shouldn't benefit from the relationship. We suspected he wanted the gifts to entice people to do deals with him, but eventually he was shamed into passing out the items.

As more and more time went by and I met Vlasov's colleagues from VTR, I began to understand him better. I grew to suspect that VTR was not a hot department for smart, ambitious young Soviets working in the Chamber of Commerce.

As I thought about the role of commercial communication in the controlled Soviet society, it dawned on me that it was quite understandable that the agency responsible for "advertising" would not be given a high standing. Until the Soviet Union began to open up to foreigners, most organized mass communication was government propaganda. Even if it wasn't for pure political purposes, it would be something like helping the government get rid of an excess of goods, urging citizens to accomplish the goals of the current five-year plan, or encouraging Soviet couples to have more children.

I hoped that Vlasov in the few years he worked at VTR recognized its shortcomings as an international agency, so that he could understand why our joint venture must be better. Unaccustomed to competition, *the* Soviet state advertising agency, VTR, had already let foreigners win some of the country's most lucrative communications contracts. The first opportunity for organizing TV advertising was awarded to the Italians—the media baron Berlusconi; control of advertising posters and displays at the airport went to an Irish company; and bus/transit advertising went to an American firm, TDI. VTR simply lacked the experience to identify money-making opportunities and to take advantage of being the home team. In the past, VTR apparently had been able to benefit from its monopoly position. Now that there was a choice, the business was going elsewhere.

Vlasov thought VTR would be his last job before retirement. He could work at a leisurely pace and in relative obscurity. So, when he was given the highly visible and important assignment with our joint venture, I think he was somewhat surprised, flattered, and perhaps frightened.

He knew for sure that our joint venture would be his last job, and I suspect that he fully intended to reap the benefits he thought should come from being part of such a venture. He probably figured there was a chance at some international travel—a big perk for Soviets—and that he would get a nice Western car and plush office, better than anything he could hope for at VTR. I'm sure he never forgave me for preventing him from getting his Volvo.

Perhaps because he expected to retire in a few years, his outlook was quite shortsighted. During one of our too frequent searches to fill the position of accountant, I told him, "I'm going to increase the salary we're offering. We need someone with good experience and someone that will stay."

"That's a waste of money. We can get someone who's young for less. It's just been bad luck before."

Vlasov wanted all the hard and soft currency kept in the bank. Although I don't know the amount of pressure on him from his superiors to start bringing in hard currency immediately, I do know he never wanted to spend any hard money. The Volvos were the only exception.

He wanted to use the cheapest Soviet furnishings for the office. When I ordered the most durable carpeting, made of our client Du Pont's Antron fiber, to stand up to Moscow winters, he objected, and wouldn't believe that in the long run the carpeting would probably end up being the least expensive. And it was the same with other office equipment and furnishings.

Mike and I operated with our typical American sense of urgency, and Vlasov found it pretty difficult to keep up. Part of it was age. Part of it was that we were demanding: We expected more tasks accomplished than he apparently was accustomed to, and faster than he could deliver. He tacitly made promises to us, then found he couldn't fulfill them. His failure to get the telex line installed was one time when I fortunately could step in and help.

Vlasov was in an awkward position. We had the same titles of co-general manager, except that I also had the title of chief executive officer. He knew that unofficially I carried much more weight: I brought the knowledge of how to run an ad agency; most of the Western clients gave us assignments because of Y&R's or Burson-Marsteller's previous involvement; and I controlled the hard currency. I'm sure he realized that he had to defer to me. Yet he kept looking for ways to exert his 50 percent influence. Probably he didn't know whether he could trust me and thus he regarded me warily.

There were a few times when he hinted broadly that I could get things done quicker if I went over his head, although he never admitted it outright. Several months after the agreement was signed, when the work on the office dragged on and there was still no hint of when Mike and I would get apartments, Vlasov said, "You need to go to Golanov yourself on this, because coming from the Americans, he'll feel a sense of pride and disappointment that his system is not delivering. You'll get a more definite answer than I can."

After those rare occasions when he was more open and honest, he would revert back to his stiff, Bolshevik style. I'm sure he gave every project his best effort. The system just wouldn't let him deliver. It wasn't a personal failure: it was the system; but he was the messenger, and that role proved a great frustration.

He wanted us to think he was more powerful within the Soviet hierarchy than he apparently was. On an official level, he was certainly high up. Theoretically, Vlasov was equivalent to the number-two person at any Y&R agency. In our agencies, the number-two man or woman can and does get things done. We expected the same sort of clout—especially since he was operating within his own system—but obviously this was a misunderstanding or naivete on our part. He was probably as effective as any bureaucrat at his level could be, but what we came to understand was that there was a big gap between the number one and number two in any organization within the Soviet Union. And since joint ventures were still relatively new, his position was even more unclear.

One time, Vlasov and I were attending a dinner meeting at a Moscow restaurant. In the men's room, we ran into Georgy Arbatov, a high-profile confidant of Gorbachev whom I had met a few times in the United States and Canada through his association with Boris Birshtein and through Ted Turner's World Peace Society.

I'll always remember Georgy's classic quip to the press when he was interviewed in Canada about McDonald's opening in Moscow. "Fast food is better than no food."

"Gary, how are you?" He greeted me warmly.

"Nice to see you again, Georgy." I turned to introduce him to Vlasov, whose mouth dropped open.

This chance encounter was a clear reminder of the Soviet sensitivity to hierarchy in this "classless society." When we got to the table, Vlasov launched into quite an animated story with Deomidov in Russian about the chance meeting. I didn't understand much except the mention several times of Arbatov's name. But the gist of the conversation and Vlasov's impression were quite clear. Strangely, we as American businessmen had more access to senior Soviets than our Soviet partners did.

Perhaps Vlasov's ineffectualness stemmed from his involvement in foreign service and living abroad. Instead of spending years in the Moscow establishment, building contacts and a personal informal network, he had maneuvered to be stationed outside the country, enjoying the good foreign life. To be truly wired into Moscow, one must have ways outside the formal channels through allies to accomplish important tasks, both professional and personal.

Despite his diplomatic experience, Vlasov was no diplomat with the Soviet staff. From his desk chair in our open office system, he would shout into the other smaller cubicles, "Roman, here in my office! Come here now!"

Roman would bolt out of his chair and race in. Or it could be Valery or Natalie. More often than not these outbursts would come just after I sat down with Vlasov to get a status report on various projects.

"Don't know. I'll have to check," was his usual answer. He delegated everything, taking personal responsibility for nothing.

As far as I could tell, Vlasov didn't use any device to monitor the progress of projects. When I asked him how we were doing on a specific project, he would get terribly upset and start shouting at whoever was working on the project. "Why isn't this finished? Where is that research?"

He never assumed responsibility himself and never helped his staff set priorities. *They* were always responsible. He made them think everything was always top priority, so staffers never knew which project to work on first.

We learned several months after starting work that the reason we lost three of our original hires—Yuriy Pintelin and Mikhail Stroykov as account directors and Galina Golantseva as our accountant—was that they didn't want to work for Vlasov, not that they had much better offers, as we had been led to believe.

Stroykov became a thorn in Vlasov's side because he started to learn that initiative paid off when he worked for us. A deadline for a Kodak assignment was fast approaching, and we reminded Stroykov that he was responsible for completing the work. As the deadline grew imminent, it was clear he couldn't finish without working overtime, unheard of in this city where extra effort is seldom rewarded.

He complained to us that he had plans the nights and weekends we expected him to be working, and we told him that was no excuse.

"The client expects this to be done. You have the assignment. You do it." I was tough with him.

Mike and I met him at the office on Sundays and stayed late with him, and when he finished he had done quite a credible job.

I rewarded him with a hearty "Good work," and a pat on the back. I also sent a memo to his personnel file, with a copy to Vlasov. No sooner was this typed and distributed than Vlasov came storming into my office.

"Never again! Don't ever do that again!" Vlasov was furious.

"What's the problem, Vladimir?"

"That's not the way we do things here. You never put things like that in someone's file. Other staffers will be resentful and jealous if you pick out one to praise."

"Well, Vlasov, when people work hard, they deserve to be recognized."

We noticed after that that every time Mike or I praised the work of one of our people, Vlasov's jaw got set real tight. The philosophy here was a convoluted version of "keeping up with Joneses." Only they tried to hold the Joneses back.

Once Mike overheard Vlasov dressing down Roman by using an old Russian proverb, something like "Your initiative, your punishment." Mike finally coaxed Pashin into explaining its meaning.

He said it represented an attitude discouraging anyone from volunteering — either ideas or themselves — unless they know the outcome, so no one is willing to come up with suggestions that might be rejected. The attitude prevailed throughout society and was ingrained starting early in grade school.

"It was like saying, 'I'm really sorry I have to whack you, but you know I have to whack you,'" Mike said.

That was a tough one for us to fight.

On rare occasions, there were a few glimmers of the kind of man Vlasov could have been under a different sort of system and in a different society. Maybe under different circumstances we could even have been friends.

Once he told me how much he loved living in — of all places — Iceland. The Soviets had a nice compound there, and Vlasov loved fishing and the out-of-doors.

He lived for the weekends, when he could do all sorts of projects at his dacha, a small wooden cabin on the outskirts of Moscow. One time I brought back from the States a do-it-yourself woodworking magazine, which he seemed to like; and on another occasion he asked me to bring him a few packets of seeds so he could plant vegetables.

I bought a packet of each kind of vegetable that I found on the seed rack, and he was overwhelmed by the assortment and variety. I couldn't have spent more than $8, but you would have thought I had given him a million dollars, he was so appreciative. I have done this for the whole staff every spring since then. It allows them to have some control over getting fresh vegetables.

The pressures on Vlasov eventually took their toll. Six weeks after we officially opened the office in October, he suffered a serious heart attack after a bitter argument with Mike about the use of cars. He was out for twelve weeks. During that time, through Pashin, he asked if I could get some heart medication for him while I was on a business trip in Germany. Apparently, his doctor felt the medicine might be helpful but it couldn't be found in Moscow. With some fast talking, I got it without a prescription from a sympathetic Munich pharmacist. Vlasov came back in against his doctor's advice. Believe it or not, I had missed him, and was happy to see him when he walked in one morning.

We sat in the conference room and chatted for at least two hours about the business over several cups of coffee.

"Do you think it would be possible for me to come back half-time?" he asked me.

"Vladimir, this job really requires full-time commitment," I told him. He was disappointed but said he understood.

"Would there be a possibility of freelance project work?"

"Yes, I'm sure we can use your expertise as a paid consultant on projects, Vladimir. Once you're ready to start working, let's talk." He chatted congenially with everyone in the office, then went home.

I went home for lunch. When I came back, Fedorov came into my office and said Vlasov had suffered another heart attack and died at his apartment. Dazed, I fell into my desk chair. I couldn't believe it. He had been sitting across the table from me just three hours earlier. He had looked quite healthy and rested. I felt bad. We had our differences, but I didn't wish him ill.

I wanted to do whatever was appropriate for Vlasov's funeral. Fedorov said there would be some sort of secular service and that he would be buried at his beloved dacha in the country. Fedorov let me know that it wouldn't be appropriate for me to attend the service. He and Pashin were the only staff people who went. The office sent flowers and some food to the family, along with our condolences. Oddly, Mike and I seemed the most upset. Vladimir was not generally liked by the staff.

Back from the service, Pashin said it would be customary for the staff to drink a round of vodka for Vladimir. We stood around the conference-room table and poured a glass for all, including one for Vladimir, which sat for forty days by custom until someone finally removed it. We wished him well and hoped for the best for his wife and children.

The office ran more smoothly without Vlasov. Pashin filled in as the senior Soviet until a permanent replacement could be named.

Vlasov's son came to the office a couple of times to clear out his things, but Mike and I were never introduced. We felt that perhaps the family blamed us for his death. Too much pressure, too many long hours, too many confrontations. I fear there is some truth in that, and I feel sad about it.

9

WHOSE STAFF IS THIS ANYWAY?

"LET'S BRING BACK A PORNO TAPE ON OUR NEXT TRIP IN. WE'LL play it all night. That will give them something interesting to listen to."

Freddye and I were having our occasional discussion about bugs one weekend evening. Was anyone listening? By November 1990 we had finally settled in as a family and were relaxing at home.

"Hey, whoever you are, what are you listening for?" I shouted at the hidden microphone.

When I first arrived in the Soviet Union, I thought about bugs a lot. I was apprehensive and very conscious of what I said on the phone and in the apartment. I didn't think much about listening devices once we moved into the office, because it was such a large open space and there were lots of noises — a difficult arrangement for listening.

"Are there really bugs?" I asked the veterans.

"Just assume everything is bugged," the people at the embassy told us.

Obviously, Vlasov thought his office phone was tapped, since he felt he lost the use of it when "someone" heard that a foreigner called him on it. When you're at someone's house, they always play the stereo very loud, presumably to drown out conversations.

It wasn't a major deal for us because we never were involved in any political issues, although from time to time I'd catch myself saying, "This is a stupid system." The listeners might not like hearing that, but I didn't think it would get me in a big deal of trouble.

Still, just on principle, the idea of someone invading my privacy, intruding on "my" space, was insulting. Mike and I were concerned during the negotiations as we discussed what points we would yield on and what ones we wouldn't. If someone heard our strategy, it would make the difficult negotiations more difficult. So we made sure we talked only in restaurants and other public places.

One day a couple of months after we first began commuting, we joked about giving our staff nicknames to confuse the listeners. "Well, I think Vlasov should be named Skippy," I told Mike. Serious and businesslike, Vlasov was the antithesis of a bouncy, bubbly Skippy. Mike burst out laughing. "That's great." His good mood was contagious, and we named them all.

The nicknames also helped us differentiate between Soviets with the same names, and there seemed to be a lot of that. For instance, we knew two Volodyas who were drivers—our own Volodya, and another driver I met before we got our office cars.

The "other" Volodya, unlike ours, spoke English fairly well. One day, he was driving Freddye and me to Izmailova

Park to look at the paintings that local artists set up every weekend in the hopes of selling their work. We were chatting as we drove away from downtown Moscow and somehow he mentioned that he was an "Afghani."

"What do you mean?" I asked him.

"Well, I fought in the war with Afghanistan."

"That's interesting. You know your country's experiences in Afghanistan have been likened in some ways to my country's in Vietnam. And I fought there."

He stopped the taxi, turned around in his seat, and embraced me. "Then we are brothers," he said as his eyes filled with tears. "We have suffered the same kind of misery, in different places and at different times, but the same kind of misery."

I didn't know what to say. He obviously felt a special kinship with me, and I liked him also. It was a moving moment that I won't forget. After our office cars came, whenever we needed an extra car, I'd call on his services. And we hired him to drive our clients during the trade show. He stayed in touch for quite a few months, checking every so often to see if we needed him; but after a while, his calls stopped, and I never found out what happened to my "brother in combat."

One day, Freddye and I were getting ready to go back to the States for a short break at Thanksgiving. As we were having dinner at home, we talked of how much we were looking forward to our trip. "You know those jars of caviar we have in the refrigerator from the office. They would make great gifts for those back in the States who have supported us," I said.

"Yeah, but that's really for jv use here as gifts. I'm not sure it would be appropriate to take that back," Freddye said.

"I don't know."

We didn't really decide and the conversation moved onto

something else. The next day, one of our Soviet employees came up to me in the office. "You know those jars of caviar. If you want to take some back, go ahead. It's okay. We'll get more. They do make great gifts."

Freddye was in the office at the time and happened to hear his comment. We exchanged glances. We both knew we just had confirmation that Big Brother had been listening.

That got me thinking, "Gee, what else do they listen to? That porno tape we've threatened to smuggle in would give them an earful. Does someone just sit around all day and listen? Or do they tape and play it back? Either way, what a boring job. It's as if there are two societies here, one living and one listening."

Yuri, our bookkeeper, clued me in that listening devices were everywhere. As we were on our way to a meeting outside the office one day, he began discussing a project. "Well, why didn't you bring this up during our meeting yesterday?"

He looked at me curiously. "Don't you know?"

"Know what?" I wasn't in the mood for Twenty Questions.

"There are some things you don't talk about in our office because you don't want others to know."

The message was penetrating.

There were other clues. When some of the Chase Bank executives redid their apartment, they took up the carpeting and found a whole network of wires underneath. They were advised to put everything back because the listeners just get mad, and the authorities return immediately to rewire. I believe the reason the Soviets want foreigners to live together in the same "expat ghetto" buildings is that it saves wire.

Mike got his own lesson. One night, Mike and a young woman working as an intern in the office were going on to an evening meeting. Mike needed to stop by his apartment to pick up some papers.

"Oh, you have a CD player," she commented admiringly as they walked in. "I've never heard one."

"Would you like to hear some jazz?" Mike asked.

"Yes, I would love that." She seemed grateful. After a few minutes of music, off they went to their meeting.

The next morning, Roman Diukarev pulled Mike aside. "If you want to take bimbos to your apartment, that's fine; nobody cares," he scolded. "But when you take a nice young professional to your apartment, you can ruin her career."

Mike was taken aback. "What do you mean?"

"You went to your apartment to listen to music last night," he accused.

"How do you know that?" Mike asked.

"I just know," Roman said.

"That's not good enough, Roman."

"Okay, okay. The listeners told me."

Mike just shook his head.

"It's okay. I had them take it off the logs because I knew there wasn't anything to it, but it still could hurt her reputation very badly."

Later, we learned that one of our female employees faced some questioning by the Mezh Hotel people once after she baby-sat for Mike's daughter Katie during her visits to Moscow. It was something they learned about through listening devices.

Our relationship with the staffers was strictly business. Whether they socialized among themselves, we weren't sure. In any public place, there is a formality—a brusqueness bordering on rudeness—among Soviets, even those who are friends. Every morning when staffers arrived, the routine was to take off their coats and then go to everyone else there and shake hands with the typical soft Soviet handshake.

Shortly after each listening incident, we'd forget about bugs and watchers. In the beginning, Mike and I would try to guess who our official watcher was. Supposedly, each joint venture had one. We were suspicious of just about every staffer at one time or another.

"You know, it's got to be Pashin or Roman," I decided. They were the two Communist Party members of the staff. Besides, Roman was very likable and worked harder than any other staffer.

Mike disagreed. "Nope, it's probably Fedorov or even Volodya, because they can always get things done. Remember Volodya circumvented six weeks worth of form-signing to get our copier installed."

"It's true, Volodya hardly ever comes back empty-handed. And neither does Fedorov."

"Maybe Volodya really understands English and pretends he doesn't so that we will speak more freely around him."

Just when we were sure we'd uncovered our watcher, something would happen and we'd change our minds.

"Maybe it's Vlasov. Maybe that's why they put him in the jv," Mike concluded.

We even suspected Natalie at one point. We never found out who was watching us, and as time passed it became less and less of an issue. Surely it was clear to all who watched and listened that we were not political . . . a little crazy maybe, but not political.

The staff was integral to getting our job done, and I didn't have time to worry about bugs, watchers, and snoops. I was too busy trying to teach the staff the basics of modern advertising and marketing.

Those who joined us had to be special people—ambitious, with a sense of adventure, and not afraid of a certain amount of risk. Working for a joint venture offered perks for sure: a nice office, use of a Western car, hard currency, and perhaps the chance to travel outside the country.

There was a downside. We would be working harder and for longer hours than any Soviet organization they would have known before. Our office wasn't conveniently located, and staffers would have a long commute on several different forms of transportation. They would be required to put in extra hours at training sessions and occasionally work evenings and weekends.

There was also the risk that if *glasnost* and *perestroika* didn't work and were reversed, and the hardliners came back into power, those who had been close to the foreigners in joint ventures could be suspect.

One of our Coudert Brothers attorneys liked to say, "There are two kinds of Soviets: One group that is embracing and pushing *perestroika,* and a second group that is taking the names of those in the first group."

In fact, some of the things we did in the normal course of business violated laws on the books, although ones that were rarely enforced. For instance, we were told by the staff that it was illegal for a Soviet to walk down the street with a foreigner alone because a citizen is not supposed to be in an isolated situation with a foreigner. This meant that neither Mike nor I could travel legally to a meeting with a client or supplier with just one of our Russian colleagues. The reasoning, relating to security in the cold war days, was that there was less chance that an individual would try to undermine the system if there was a witness. Our embassy had the same rules for government employees, although it didn't apply to private individuals like us.

We weren't involved in anything politically or militarily sensitive, so we basically ignored regulations like those.

Many people thought they would be removed from the books soon anyway.

As the staff came together, it became apparent quite soon that Roman was a treasure. From the beginning, whatever assignments we gave him—research, trade shows, PR coordination—he did them well, on time, and asked for more.

He also grew into serving in an unofficial capacity as an envoy from me to the Soviet staff, and vice versa. This was a role that came about without any planning or foresight. There were certain messages that simply couldn't be conveyed through Vlasov.

Roman would idle into my office, arrange his medium-size, somewhat paunchy frame comfortably against the door frame, smile, and start to chat. Soft-spoken and discreet, he sported a walrus-style mustache and thick, longish hair. His easy manner, excellent English, and ready wit said: "Trust me."

Our amiable conversations would take on the appearance of a casual chat, but during them he'd pass along the concerns of the Soviet staff in an informal way, giving me insight into morale and the mood and tempo of the office. Once, he made sure I knew how important a refrigerator was so that the staff could bring their lunch and store a supply of snacks and drinks.

In the original office, we were to have had a kitchen, which is customary in Moscow. Someone often comes in and prepares a meal at noon for the staff. When we ended up in the Mezh, there was no kitchen and cooking was prohibited. It wasn't a big thing for me. In fact, I didn't even think twice about it; but Roman let me know it was important to the staff, because eating lunch out even in the ruble staff restaurant provided in the Sovincenter was very hard on their budgets.

The messages went both ways. I could let him pass along

my concern at certain tasks not being accomplished without having to make a big scene with a staffer. Like getting in time sheets on time and keeping the cars clean.

In his official capacity, Roman progressed rapidly. He was such a quick study that we soon named him account director on J&J and General Electric. As part of his training, we wanted him to experience life in the West firsthand and to see the actual workings of a market economy. Although he had been an army officer and military interpreter, his assignments outside the Soviet Union had taken him only to Ethiopia. So, we planned a trip for him to America as soon as we could spare him from setting up the office. I would have liked to have been by his side when he got his introduction to the West.

Just after the official office opening in October 1989, Roman left for a week's visit to Y&R's office in Cedar Rapids, Iowa. The office, known as CMF&Z, was designated as our sister agency just as it was to the Beijing office. Its size and style were appropriate to ours, and Iowans seem to go out of their way to help anyone. Y&R in New York, the world's biggest ad agency, is great, but our many small requests could get lost.

"Your one week will be worth six months of training here," I told him. "You'll see a market economy in action. See choice on the shelves and see advertising in many kinds of media."

We wanted his trip to be special personally, and we arranged for him to stay with Buzz Baker, the CMF&Z president. Roman would benefit from living with a typical family and seeing how they spent their time at play as well as at work. He would also be able to save his per diem for gifts.

During the fall, Buzz is the official announcer at the local high school football games, where his son played. At half-time, Buzz gave Roman a celebrity introduction over the loud speaker. As Roman made his way onto the field, he was stunned by the crowd's cheers and applause. He quickly recovered and responded with a big grin, his arms high above his head. The event was hard-core Americana: hot dogs, marching band, pom-pom girls, and Midwest good-will.

Throughout the week, Roman's celebrity status grew. He was welcomed as a speaker at an elementary school and made an honorary guest at Buzz's country club. That allowed him to accept the gift of an insignia blazer. He was written up in the local paper.

One day as the family was finishing dinner, the doorbell rang. As Buzz opened the door, Roman heard shouts of "Trick or treat!" and in walked kids in colorful costumes. Roman's puzzled expression gave way to a hearty laugh as the family explained the tradition of Halloween in America.

By week's end, he was quite dazzled by the attention from the citizens of Cedar Rapids. Although he stopped off in Chicago and New York, Roman came home praising that very special place in America — Cedar Rapids.

A couple of months later, we were opening the mail at the agency and found a videotape from Buzz of the season's highlights of the Cedar Rapids football team. Everyone in the agency stopped working to watch Roman being cheered by the crowd. They chimed in, too, as proud of the honor as he was.

After that trip, Roman began asking me even more questions about America. Our car trips turned into sessions where he would grill me. "How much does a house cost? How do you finance a house that costs that much? How do you get life insurance? How does it work?"

At one point, I worried that he was thinking about defecting. Then I decided he was simply hungry to know the workings of a capitalistic society.

He confessed that his real dream was to work in an agency in America and then return to his native Tallinn, the capital of Estonia, to open a Y&R branch office there. If the agency business develops in this part of the world and if Roman grows with it, there's no reason why he can't fulfill his dream some day.

His enthusiasm and ambition set a good example for others on staff, especially Natalie. She had gone from secretary to office manager to account exec within six months. We put Roman and Natalie together on J&J to form a good, hard-working team.

We nicknamed them "the Bickersons" because they were always arguing in order to perfect their work. She was very strong-willed, opinionated, and smart. They would get into the damnedest debates about . . . well, anything. They bickered as if they were married.

Both thought they were experts with English and would nitpick over a translation word by word. On o.b. tampons, I generally sided with Natalie. "She's got more experience than you in this category, Roman," I said. "But on baby products, you're the expert, since you have a baby at home."

One day I got a call from our Cedar Rapids office with a simple translation assignment. They were pitching the Square D business worldwide and needed a translation for a short, memorable slogan indicating "We respond quickly." The company, heavily involved in industrial electrical equipment and electronic components, was using it with the picture of a fast big cat, either a jaguar, cheetah, or leopard.

Russian is a complicated language, with intricate subtleties and many choices of words. Even so, I was amazed at the three-hour debate between Roman and Natalie over whether the wording should be "We respond instantaneously," or "We respond like lightning," or "We're here right now," or any of some twenty-five other slogan options they had come up with.

Natalie argued that we could not use the cheetah at all. "Leopards and cheetahs are considered bad animals. They'll have to dump the animal."

"Forget it, Natalie. Everyone knows Square D is a Western firm. We're not going to lose the cat," Mike volunteered.

Natalie is a purist and understands shades of meaning extremely well, but she gets hung up on the rules.

"Look, Natalie, we're not writing a treatise or *War and Peace*. Sometimes you have to bend the language a bit. And as long as it's understandable and people aren't turned off, then it's okay," Mike explained.

Roman doesn't have the same level of understanding and command of the language, but he doesn't get hung up on formalities. Mike called this a lesson in the "commercial familiar."

Natalie blossomed, training a replacement as she moved up the ladder. Within a year, she had risen to a position where she was "needed" to make a business trip to Germany to check the type on the package and instructions for o.b. tampons before printing.

"We really shouldn't print a million of those boxes without a final check that they're correct," Heinz Schmidt said with a twinkle in his eye. "Natalie, would you mind making that trip for us?"

She jumped out of her chair. "Yes! Yes! I'll be happy to go." Dr. Schmidt and I had planned this trip as a reward for all of her good work on the project.

I marveled at the work ethic and drive of Soviet women, clearly harder workers than the men. They struggle in an extremely chauvinistic society. The women get up early, get the kids off to school, work all day, stand in line for several hours for food before going home, prepare dinner, take care of the kids, wash the laundry, clean the apartment, fall into bed, get up early, and start the process all over again. They have tough lives.

Natalie never talked about her personal life. She was an incurable romantic, loved Dustin Hoffman, and dreamed about a medical miracle that would magically help her shed a few pounds at the same time she was savoring every bite of a gourmet meal. In her thirties, she was old not to be married. She was warm, energetic, quick, and at times quite funny. In appearance she sometimes reminded me of the tennis star Steffi Graf.

Rejecting the terrible life around her, she must have decided that succeeding professionally was worth the sacrifice of marriage.

"Call me Natalie," she'd remind anyone who called her Natasha. Vlasov refused to Westernize her name. When I slipped, she glared with those steely gray eyes.

Roman stood out because our only other male account director, Valery Fedorov, was a remarkable contrast in both personality and accomplishment. Mikhail Stroykov—the tall, slim Soviet we hired as an account director—lasted only a very short time because he refused to accept Vlasov's dictatorial style. When "Stretch," as we had nicknamed him, found a job with another joint venture in town, we never got around to replacing him.

So here we had industrious Roman and wheeler-dealer Fedorov. Initially I was enthusiastic about Fedorov because he was so well connected in official Moscow. Although he was of medium height and in his forties, he had the posture of a much older man. His complexion and hair were dark, and he frequently grumbled to himself, shaking his head.

As time passed, I became more suspicious of Fedorov's methods and wondered where he spent most of his time, because he was rarely at his desk and even less frequently involved in any productive work for the agency. After some time, I realized that we could get things done ourselves simply because we were becoming a well-respected joint venture. In assignments that didn't require connections, Fedorov's performance was barely acceptable. He missed deadlines. He always had excuses why something wasn't done. He didn't follow up on his own. Only when he sat behind the wheel of our company cars did he become aggressive, in fact, so aggressive that the cars ended up needing repairs several times after he'd driven them.

We asked him to arrange for a photographer at an event so that we could include photos with a press kit to be sent out immediately afterward. Weeks passed before the photos were ready. At trade shows, he would show up late to put up displays.

To make sure his poor English skills weren't the reason for his difficulties, Mike and I asked Pashin to translate assignments into Russian. Still there was no improvement.

One weekend I walked into the office to find the conference room filled with strangers, smoking and drinking the office's beer. In the midst of them was Fedorov.

"Who are they?" I motioned to him.

"Oh, they're from Yugoslavia. We're about to sign a lumber contract."

"No contracts that I don't see. This is a joint venture and I'm CEO." As usual, Fedorov was looking for the big, one-time get-rich deal that would set him up for life. He had no interest in advertising.

After Vlasov suffered his heart attack, Fedorov confiscated Vlasov's office and pretended it was his. He desperately wanted to be a big shot, but wasn't willing to pay his dues. We wrestled to train and motivate him for more than a year, but finally told him it wasn't going to work. Firing someone in the Soviet Union is almost unheard of, and it took us some time to get rid of this nonworker in the workers' paradise.

Once the official opening and board meeting were behind us, we started regular training sessions every Tuesday and Thursday mornings at seven-thirty sharp.

"How do we start?" I asked, as Mike and I began to work out our curriculum.

"We've got to make it simple and somehow make it real," Mike said.

We remembered an animated film we'd seen back in the mid-seventies that we thought would convey an important lesson. Amoco, the oil company, produced two very good videos called *The Kingdom of Mocha* and *Return to Mocha*. In the form of educational films about free enterprise, their original purpose was a well-disguised plea to convince the feds to leave oil companies alone.

The films were set on a little island called Mocha, where everybody lived well in a simple economy. Every Mochaite had a special skill. One was an excellent fisherman, one knew how to grow bananas, and so forth. Each person traded his goods for those he needed, and everyone was healthy. As time went on, the citizens became impatient with all the trading. So they developed a medium of exchange—a currency— to replace barter. That led to trading with other islands. And so the films illustrated simply and clearly how a free market economy developed. We used them to great success in one of our first training sessions to introduce the basic idea of free enterprise.

The training sessions progressed. "What is a customer?" "What is a client?" we asked. The Soviets lack any familiarity with the concept of service. Then we'd say, "Clients come first. Our business revolves around clients. This is a service business. We are here to help clients by giving them the communications they need to accomplish their business objectives."

This was not an easy concept for them to understand because in a centrally controlled economy, there is no incentive to work hard and please customers. With no competition and shortages of everything, customers had no choice but to return, no matter how badly they were treated.

Mike spent a whole session talking about time sheets. "That's what we get paid for. Our time is what we sell," he explained.

Getting the staff to fill out the sheets remained a problem until one day I instructed the bookkeeper not to pass out paychecks until time sheets were completed.

"Look, Y&R's books are open at all times to clients," I explained time and again to the staff. "If clients want to come in and examine how much time each staffer spends on their business, they're welcome. It's the only documentation we have to show that we're providing the work we're charging for. You must have your time documented to show a client they're getting what they're paying for." I don't know if the concept sank in, but when paychecks were withheld, the time sheets got filled out.

In other sessions, we asked what is a customer. "We need to know who our clients' customers are, what they think. The customer's age, income, education, sex; where the customer lives, works. The customer's media habits. Is the customer an achiever, a leader, a risk taker, conservative?"

Living under a system with a tradition of hidden microphones and secret police, our staffers expressed doubts about whether they could get accurate information. So we talked about research, how to gather and analyze data.

In other sessions, we'd watch and critique commercials. "Just give me the opportunity to buy some of these things here!" Natalie looked longingly at all the plentiful Western goods.

We also sprinkled in some lectures on responsibility. I'm not sure what kind of an impression they made because once Pashin just didn't show up when he had an important assignment due. When we couldn't reach him on the phone, we sent someone to his apartment to look for him.

It turned out that he had suffered a minor welding accident and had gone to a clinic. A burst of flame had scorched his skin, but luckily his eyes weren't harmed. He apparently thought that was enough of an excuse not to show up. I had no problem with his going to the clinic, but I did get upset that he did not call in.

After a couple of other similar incidents of no-shows, particularly around deadline time, we realized that it was not unusual in this society to think that falling ill is an acceptable excuse for not completing some work or being at a critical meeting. "Whew, I'm off the hook!" is the common reaction.

"Being sick is okay," I drummed into the staff. "Getting sick and not being in touch is *not* okay.

"It's also okay to ask for help with a project, but the time to do that is several weeks before it's due, *not* right on deadline. We all work together, and we'll help each other out." Sometimes I felt like a schoolteacher.

There's an explanation of the Russian psyche that makes a lot of sense in thinking about their work ethic. The explanation goes like this: The Russians are tied very closely to the land. In an agrarian society in this kind of climate, people work very explosively for a short period of time, and then they collapse. There's mud in the fields until the end of April, then crops must be sown quickly to make sure they're in the ground so that they have enough time to complete their growing cycle during a short growing season.

After that period, the people spend the rest of the summer recuperating: quite a contrast to the experience of the American farmer, who works hard all summer. Then the autumn with its harvest season arrives, and there's a similar situation. The crops must be reaped or they'll freeze. So again it's an explosive effort.

At Y&R/Sovero, we had deadlines to meet that required an explosive effort, but we never had much down time because we would go from one project to the next and typically work on more than one project at a time. The staff had never seen such a pace. They couldn't believe they wouldn't get a chance to rest.

Whenever we had visitors from Y&R, we lassoed them into leading a discussion or training session. We talked about how you make money on advertising, about advertising and the law, and media selections. As part of our training sessions and part of our effort to get close to the Gosteleradio people, I invited Luc Deleersnyder to come to Moscow. Luc, who ran Y&R in Brussels, had been instrumental in helping the Flemish TV station convert from a state-funded operation to a commercial station, supported by advertising. He could be valuable to the Soviets, who were exploring that same process for their television network.

For Gosteleradio, Luc prepared a daylong presentation to explain the process of commercialization. He showed commercials, discussed rate cards, and answered their questions. The next morning, he met with our staff in the conference room during a regular training session. He showed a variety of commercials that his agency had created for clients, explaining why they were done the way they were and the results they achieved.

One recurring subject at our training sessions was "choice." It's so hard to teach that concept in a land of scarcity. How can you make a point about choosing among so many brands within a single product category when people can't find any products on store shelves?

One day, Mike gave one of our interns, Tanya, a copy of the *Utne Reader*. After reading one article on environmental issues, she asked Mike to explain a section on disposable diapers.

"I understand the words, and I understand there's a serious problem with waste. But this seems very strange and unreal. We can't even buy disposable diapers, and you have magazines writing about problems of getting rid of them!"

I was torn between two opposite emotions: fear that seeing so much abundance would create tremendous dissatisfaction, and hope that seeing a better life would encourage them to work to make their own system better.

"Someday, your shelves are going to be filled here, too," I encouraged them.

"I truly hope so," Natalie responded. Others were less optimistic.

As our sessions progressed, we tackled more difficult topics: They wanted to know how to use bank checks and credit cards, and how the stock market works. "That's a tough one," I allowed.

One of the most interesting training sessions was role playing that we got the Coke account. I came in one morning: "Hi, ya'll. How are ya? My name's J. B. Coke. I'm from Atlanta, Georgia. I'm gonna give ya'll my bizness. Here's the deal. Ya got five million to spend. We operate only west of the Urals. We have only one plant and produce only three million cases the first year. No more. I wanna show those

Pepsi guys. Now, whatcha gonna do for me? I'll be back in a couple days."

J. B. Coke left.

The staffers pondered how to help Coke catch up the twenty years they were behind Pepsi.

Then, switching roles, I said: "Now what are we going to do? We have a chance to win the Coke account. Very prestigious for a fledgling agency in the Soviet Union." I saw many blank faces.

"Well, we're going to do some ads," one staffer ventured.

"First, we need to do research." Roman always seems to come up with the right answer.

"That's a great idea. What do you want to know?"

"First, we need to know if Soviets know the name 'Coke' and what kind of product it is. If not, we've got to start building brand recognition." Roman lived up to his reputation as a star.

We shuffled the staff and assigned each one a different republic. Since Roman was from Estonia, he got the Baltics; someone else was familiar with Kiev, so that person got the Ukraine.

"Pretend you've been researching this project for two weeks. Then come back in half an hour with your results."

"Huh, how's that possible?" They were puzzled.

"Make it up. That's not how we'll do it for a client, but make your best guesses since you know those regions."

I asked Roman to present first. He talked about Pepsi, how it was perceived. How often people drank it and on what occasions. Where people bought it, which people were heavy users.

"Good, Roman." I was impressed. The others followed with varying degrees of success.

"Okay. Now, for the next session on Thursday, you guys come back and make your recommendations to Mr. Coke."

Frankly, I was disappointed that they didn't take any initiative and get together after hours to prepare a presentation. But the next session proved worthwhile anyway.

We talked about whether there was enough commonality among the republics for a single campaign, or if we had to prepare five different campaigns. How would we allocate the $5 million among advertising, public relations, and sampling? How would we reach the young people? Is there a rock-'n'-roll radio station?

"No, no such thing in this country," Fedorov said emphatically as if to say, "See, you can't do things the same here."

"Well, let's start one," I said.

Their eyes bugged out. "No one has ever done anything like that!" one staffer exclaimed.

"We couldn't," another concurred.

"Why not?" I asked.

"No one would approve it," they said sadly.

Except for Roman and Natalie, the staffers refused to take any chances. The years living under repression had taken a toll on this whole generation. Can I attribute their reticence to fear? Were they afraid even to ask permission to try something new, I wondered.

I wanted to send them all out to the West to enjoy the high of a good bookstore, good video store, good cable TV, good supermarket, good choices. I wanted them to demand an efficient, people-serving system without fear and restrictions.

"You know, Mike, I can't get over how hard brainstorming is for such bright people. I never realized that standing up to put forth an idea can be so uncomfortable."

"You're pushing them to dream, to imagine things," Mike responded.

"I hope this dream doesn't turn into a nightmare for all of us," I said uneasily. I knew I was pushing the staff to the extent of their capabilities. I just hoped they could handle it.

10

BATTLE OF THE ALEXES

"GARY, LOOK AT THIS FAX! THEY'RE SAYING WE'RE NOT THE FIRST agency to open here. How could they!" One of the staffers thrust the fax just off the machine into my hands, and the others gathered round.

"These are lies, all lies," someone else chimed in.

"Now, calm down, calm down. Let's see what this is all about." I was happy to see the pride our Soviet staff were taking in their accomplishments, but I didn't want them to get so worked up they couldn't concentrate on their projects for the day.

Actually, this was the revival of a debate that had started the very day we announced that we had signed a letter of intent to enter the Soviet Union, long before we had any staff at all. The minute our announcement of an intended joint venture appeared in the Western press, a handful of other agencies felt compelled to disclose their thus far "secret" deals, each claiming that they in fact were first. Now we were getting messages over the fax from the New York office about these outrageous claims in the press.

From an operating standpoint, we didn't much care about such claims. "This is all silly," I said one day to Mike. "We know we are really first to provide services."

From a corporate image and credibility standpoint, it was important that we got the credit we were due. The claims of being first boiled down to a game of splitting hairs.

After our first few meetings with Vneshtorgreklama, we essentially were committed to a deal. So, while the attorneys and negotiators worked out the fine points, we on the operating side were going ahead with our plans just as if all contracts were signed. In other words, from my standpoint, we were actually *working* in the Soviet Union long before other companies whose paperwork showed they were "officially" here.

"It's true that we don't have certain official documents approved as soon as we hoped — or as soon as other agencies," I explained to a reporter who asked me whether we were "official" or not.

"You know, the Soviet Union is notorious for delay after delay since the wheels grind slowly under the weighty bureauracy. The true test is clients. We have clients giving us real assignments. I don't think other agencies can legitimately make that claim, and we *are* getting paid."

It was only from a publicity standpoint that it mattered whether the official documents were signed. We knew that everything official would happen eventually. But somehow other advertising agencies got some sort of satisfaction in claiming that they had beat us.

Of all of these, the most politically sensitive was Ogilvy & Mather's boast of doing us one better — not political from the government/international relations standpoint, but from the agency/business standpoint. It was a classic old-fashioned rivalry between two long-standing former colleagues, my boss Alex Kroll, and the head of Ogilvy's international division, Alex Brody.

Brody was a larger-than-life kind of guy in the ad business. Having spent thirty-two years at Young & Rubicam before joining Ogilvy just a year before all the activity started in the Soviet Union, he was one of a rare breed of admen who felt as much at home with the Japanese and the French as he did with Americans. He understood other cultures and was well admired and respected far beyond his homeland. As the Johnny Appleseed of Y&R, he had traveled the world, opening offices to strengthen the worldwide network and spread the Y&R way of doing business.

Alex Kroll, meanwhile, made just as big a name for himself on the creative side. For years the two rising stars were making parallel moves up the ladder at Y&R, heading on a course that meant an inevitable collision.

The two men had much in common. Both had ties to Eastern Europe: Brody's family roots were in Hungary, Kroll's in Poland. Both had educations grounded in America's Northeast, and both were "men for all seasons" — well-educated and sophisticated intellectuals. Kroll graduated from Rutgers after a stint at Yale, and Brody is a Princeton alum.

Their interests and talents remain broad to this day. Brody is a classical music scholar; he speaks numerous languages; he's a student of poetry, art, and philosophy. Kroll combined his academic endeavors with football, a sport that honored him as all-American.

As the number of choice positions at Y&R grew fewer with their upward climb, the two headed toward a showdown, vying for the same jobs at the top of the pyramid. Finally, it happened. In 1983, Kroll was named president of the parent company. A miffed Brody, who had spearheaded Y&R's international expansion for more than a decade, left to become a consultant. But not for long. Within a year, he was lured back to head Y&R's new joint venture with the giant Japanese agency Dentsu.

As chief executive officer of DYR (as the joint venture was known), Brody did not officially report to Kroll. There was an uneasy truce that lasted five years, until Brody left again — this time to do for Ogilvy & Mather what he had done for Y&R, build a strong international presence.

So, when the two agencies began to stake out claims on who was first in Russia just a year after Brody joined Ogilvy, there was much history and pride involved, far more than appeared on the surface.

Kroll had other motivations, too. His predecessor as head of our agency, Ed Ney, had made a tremendous contribution to establishing Y&R as one of the world's great ad agencies. He did it by developing a business that catered to his belief that a great agency must offer its clients "the whole egg" — a total communications package, not only advertising but sales promotion, public relations, direct response, and corporate design, all under the same roof. He spent much of his tenure developing all those businesses under the Young & Rubicam corporate umbrella. Today, almost all major agencies have adopted the same philosophy.

Ed Ney also took credit for the opening of the agency's first office in the Communist world — in Beijing — done under his watch, but executed by Alex Brody during his DYR days.

So I believe Kroll saw Eastern Europe and the Soviet Union in particular as his opportunity to leave his stamp on Y&R, which would be forever remembered as part of the Kroll legacy. The fact that the region played a role in his cultural heritage was an even greater attraction. In a way, I was living out his fantasy. Had there been any way for him to be the person to open the office in Moscow himself, I was convinced he would have been there to do the job.

Throughout the negotiations, it was clear that Kroll was intent on making the deal with Vneshtorgreklama work because that was our best chance of getting in fast and first. While he was open to other potential joint venture partners, his message to me was, "Get our deal finalized."

As I set out to accomplish Kroll's plan, Ogilvy was busy doing a different kind of deal, one that got the agency into Moscow through a back door. Ogilvy's claim to being first was based on the fact that the agency signed a joint venture with a Hungarian agency that had an existing arrangement with a Soviet agency.

"That doesn't count. They don't really have O&M expatriate people on the ground here," my staff argued.

"The rivalry makes a good story," I told them. "You're getting a taste of what freedom of speech and competition are all about." I was somewhat amused at the whole thing, and if it weren't that our credibility was on the line, I would have dismissed the affair entirely. As far as competition for Western accounts was concerned, Ogilvy simply wasn't a factor.

"But people will think they're running an office just like we are." Our staffers seemed plagued by the issue.

"Yes, they did get their name on a door. But that's *all* they got. They bought their way in," I said, trying to placate them.

When American clients came to Moscow, if they came directly to our offices from the airport, they didn't realize that we were unique for this city where you were lucky to have space, much less supplies and equipment that worked. If they visited other offices before ours, they realized they were seeing a minor miracle when they entered our comfortable, modern, clean, and well-equipped Western-style quarters.

As they opened the door, they were greeted by Elena's pretty smile and a warm "Good morning. Welcome to Y&R/Sovero." Quite a contrast to the gruff, rude reception they'd get elsewhere. To their right, they'd see modern chairs in fire engine red, where visitors were directed to wait for appointments. They could read relatively recent Western magazines if they wished. Comfortably interspersed throughout the reception area were our much-coveted copier, three Macintosh computer stations, telex, fax, and some video equipment.

Unlike most Moscow offices, ours was bright—the cheerful atmosphere created by white walls, simple and clean lines, good lighting, and a sense of openness throughout. Without exception, visitors would crane their necks to look beyond the reception area; almost without exception, we'd invite them for a tour. Directly behind the reception area was our only enclosed room, used primarily for meetings and conferences. Dominated by a laminate-covered oval conference table that seated ten, the room also held a TV, $1/2$-inch and $3/4$-inch multi-system video equipment, a slide projector and overhead projector stored neatly in a white laminate wall unit, a refrigerator, and a movie screen that pulled down from the ceiling. Ten chairs, upholstered in a rough-textured muted purple fabric that picked up one of the flecks in the mostly gray carpet, were set round the table.

Next to the conference room, a row of four "executive" offices—for me, Vlasov, Mike, and Pashin—lined the wall along the windows. Seven-foot-high, powder blue, fabric-covered partitions separated the offices—each compactly designed, with a built-in imitation-wood desk and white laminate hanging shelving and cabinets. A comfortable desk chair—once again in fire engine red—brought a splash of color to each executive office.

On the opposite side of the entire office space, along the wall shared with the outside hallway, five smaller but similarly furnished carrels formed well-lit work spaces for the staff, leaving enough room for another computer station in the far corner. Down the middle, tall storage and filing cabinets, as well an area for the best collection of Western periodicals in Moscow, separated the two rows of offices by creating a central divider.

When we led visitors down one aisle and up the other, we could tell which ones had seen other Soviet offices because they looked like children in F. A. O. Schwarz, wide-eyed and disbelieving.

I'm convinced our well-designed space helped us win business. We even came close to winning Ogilvy's prize account, American Express, because the local representative was so impressed by us and not so entirely confident in the promises made by Ogilvy's staff, which consisted solely of Soviets.

"I know I'm supposed to work with O&M as we do elsewhere," the Amex rep told me. "But those guys just don't understand." It wasn't simply their typically shabby offices that turned off Western clients; it was their inability to convey a thorough knowledge and vocabulary of Western marketing. So, for the first year, we pretty much felt we had the market to ourselves. No one could come close to what we offered Western clients.

Even potential Soviet clients came to us, although we lost the Gosteleradio TV job that I wanted so very much—to Saatchi & Saatchi. I believe the British agency won that business, even though they didn't have a Moscow office, because they agreed with Gosteleradio that ad rates for TV programs should be set high in view of the tremendous number of people who watch the national channels.

In the West, television rates generally are based on viewership. The more viewers, the higher the rate. But in the Soviet Union viewers didn't have much choice of programming; normally only three or four channels, depending on where they lived—two national channels, an educational channel, and local channels in Moscow and Leningrad. Furthermore, there are no sophisticated measuring services, and estimates of the number of viewers are just that—estimates. More important, marketers don't really need to advertise their products to encourage sales because anything worthwhile that appears on retail shelves disappears in a matter of hours.

So, our recommendation to Gosteleradio was to keep rates low until products began to appear, or until Western companies began to introduce themselves via corporate ad messages. Then they could gradually start increasing rates as the marketplace developed and competition heated up. But the mentality of trying to earn a quick buck without delivering value won out, and Saatchi's proposition earned our competition the assignment. It gave us little satisfaction when Gosteleradio couldn't find any takers for commercials because the rates were so high. The poor advice simply made Gosteleradio and other Soviet organizations more wary of "those fancy Western ad agencies."

"Is that going to hurt us?" I asked Mike one day after I realized what was happening.

"Probably not, but I don't feel good about it. It gives our whole industry a black eye."

One day about a year after we started up, Bert Polishook, who ran IBM, pulled me aside at a Saturday embassy brunch. "Hey, I ran into a competitor of yours."

"We don't have any competition," I said, laughing.

"Well, you do now. Somebody from BBDO came by to see me. They said they're setting up offices here."

That was the first I heard that Moscow's Madison Avenue was starting to get crowded.

"Yeah, he came to see me, too," chimed in Fred Drake, who ran General Electric's U.S.S.R. operation. They were having fun with me, but still I was surprised.

Later that day I heard the BBDO guy had been to see Du Pont as well. I was concerned since Du Pont was an account that both Y&R and BBDO served in the United States, and G.E. and IBM were accounts that Burson-Marsteller shared with BBDO.

"I guess I should try and meet our competition," I allowed, still a bit surprised that anyone else was moving here.

Shocked and pissed off, I didn't want to share the Soviet market with any other agency after all our hard work and frustration. This country, despite being home to 280 million people spread over twelve time zones and covering one-sixth of the world's landmass, wasn't big enough for more of us yet.

Sure enough, Bruce Macdonald turned up one Saturday at the embassy brunch. A pleasant fellow in his mid-fifties, he was working out of the old Ukraine Hotel for the time being, negotiating the details of a joint venture with a printing company, Vneshtorgizdat. His wife wisely remained in England while he went through the tough process of finding an apartment and office space.

"Welcome to the Big Cabbage." As we shook hands, we were cordial but eyed each other warily.

"I'm excited about being here. It's a big challenge," he said.

"That's what we all say at the beginning," I thought to myself. But rather than seem too empathetic, I told him, "That's an understatement. How are things going?"

"Slow, but you know about all that."

Indeed I did, and when I saw him again sometime later

after he had had a particularly frustrating week, I couldn't help but gloat inwardly when he said, "I guess you know how hard it is to get anything done around here. I think we've finally found office space, but I can't get our phones installed. They just keep promising."

"Oh, it's difficult all right. Just hang in there." I chuckled to myself.

MacDonald seemed like a nice guy, but I wanted Y&R/Sovero to be the only game in town as long as possible. I knew the competition would come eventually, but by then I wanted to be so far ahead that no one could catch us. Entering the Soviet Union the way we did with Westerners living here was expensive and had entailed a major commitment of agency resources, people, and money. I wasn't sure how many agency managements would be willing to make that investment. For Y&R, the investment was worth it if we could gain a big competitive advantage and the market economy developed. It was the kind of long-term investment that a privately held company could make, but that would be difficult for a publicly held company, which needs to show short-term results.

Much of it, like the ad agency business everywhere, is client-driven: when your major clients enter a new market, you'd better be there for them or risk losing the business to another agency. So, I can't say that I was surprised when Mike told me about some visitors one day.

"Things are getting pretty interesting around here. You'll never guess who dropped in while you were gone," he began.

"So, who did I miss this time? Someone with a hotel deal?"

"No, we had some curious guests that work at McCann-Erickson. They looked like they were very impressed with our digs here."

Like Y&R, McCann is one of the top ten international agencies in the world. Although Y&R is larger, McCann probably has more offices in more places than any other agency, mostly to service Coca-Cola, which is sold in over a hundred countries. Probably without exception, McCann represents Coca-Cola in all those places where it's sold, and that accounts for hundreds of millions of dollars of business for the agency.

So, as Coca-Cola looked to start up in the Soviet Union, McCann obviously needed to be here. What made the situation sticky for them was that Burson-Marsteller — our PR arm and the place that Mike came from — also represented Coke in a public relations function. So Coke was Mike's client, too.

From time to time, Coca-Cola execs were in and out of our offices, and since they didn't have an ad agency here, we helped them run some ads that McCann created back in the States.

"The McCann guys must have heard about that little project a few months ago," Mike said.

"You mean when we helped Coke participate in the McDonald's opening?"

"Yeah, that one."

"Why's that?" I asked.

"Well, they came strolling in, and they said they were happy to know we were supporting *their* client. I told them, 'Happy to do it. They're our client too,'" Mike said.

"They didn't sound very grateful, and they said, 'You should know that we're going to open up here soon and we'll take charge of the account. We appreciate your help during this interim period,' and the emphasis was definitely on *interim*."

Mike simply told them, "Okay, guys. Good luck."

What probably worried them most was that while Mike

wore his Burson hat to handle Coke's PR, the name on the door was not Burson-Marsteller, it was Y&R.

McCann's alleged presence had given us a scare once before. On our first trip to Moscow in 1988, as Mike and I walked through the Mezh, we saw a giant electrical signpost in the multi-story atrium advertising McCann-Erickson Moscow as part of a worldwide agency network with 144 offices in 67 countries. The sign, in both English and Russian, listed a local phone number. Mike and I were surprised and worried that we had competition even before we started.

So Mike phoned to see what he could find out. The person who answered said in very broken English, "I'm a rep. Just a rep. You have serious business? I give you number to call. In Frankfurt."

And that was the last we'd heard of McCann-Erickson until this visit. Later, I read that they signed up in a joint venture with Novosti, a Soviet news service. Ad agencies often ended up picking partners that made for strange matches in totally unrelated businesses — even banks and financial services — just for the sake of expedience and in the hope of being awarded high-level government contacts.

Lots of agencies sent representatives over to check out the territory, but most went back quite discouraged. Technically, our biggest competition should have been Soyuztorgreklama, the state agency that handled all domestic advertising until rigid regulations were relaxed. This was also the agency that was part of the multi-country deal Ogilvy signed with the Hungarians. So the rivalry of the Alexes loomed large. But not much actually materialized. Although Soyuztorgreklama had many offices and lots of staff, it didn't have the know-how. Thus, despite our fears, we never faced any real competition during my entire tenure.

We heard rumors that D'Arcy Masius Benton & Bowles,

another big multi-national agency, was being forced to open an office in Moscow by their client Procter & Gamble, but we never saw anyone. We did see Murray Smith from Bozell in the Mezh one morning.

"Nice to see a familiar face," he greeted us. "We've been 'in-country' for several days" — referring to the colleagues he was traveling with.

They looked it, pale, drawn, weary. I knew that feeling. It's almost impossible to camouflage the distress and weariness that accompany the shock of one's initial trips. I invited them to our office to look around. I figured that seeing our new place after dragging around town looking at awful space would really discourage them if everything else hadn't. I admit to being devious. I guess my tactics weren't necessary because they didn't show up.

In trying to find space, ad agencies like ours were competing with all kinds of other service businesses — law and accounting firms, for example. Like us, Coudert Brothers took a risk, made an investment, and sent two top people: Richard Dean and Mark Vecchio. They too were enjoying the fruits of being the first and best. When I reflected on our year's worth of accomplishments, the Battle of the Alexes and all the other battles seemed worthwhile.

11

LIVING IT UP

"Hey, Mike, how about shooting some hoops? Maybe we can even find a pickup game." It was a Sunday afternoon when I picked up the phone to call Mike. For the first time, I was in Moscow over a weekend and not pressed to get some project finished.

Freddye wasn't with me yet, and frankly, I could use some exercise after the past nonstop work week. The walls in the apartment were closing in. Aloneness was becoming a big issue. After I hung up, I felt a little embarrassed. Did I sound like a kid calling up his best buddy? Mike laughed when I told him my thoughts. "Was it okay that two senior ad execs were running down to the embassy to 'play'?" I posed that question aloud but I didn't expect an answer.

Quickly, I put aside my reservations. Anyone who persevered here deserved some fun when and where they could find it. I gave another private thanks to Mike Mears and his efforts to give us businessmen an escape, even though there weren't many options. The embassy offered a terrific workout room, but today I felt like combining exercise with some socializing. Mike and I jogged the few blocks to the embassy and enjoyed a good workout, including a hotly contested squash match.

The embassy fulfilled several roles, including that of social planner. Its most successful events were those that included spouses. The best part of the week was the Saturday-morning brunches. That was also the time we usually traded coveted newspapers and magazines.

Soon after I began commuting between New York and Moscow, I asked one of the expats at the brunch, "What do you do when you're not working?"

"There aren't many choices, but someone usually hosts a dinner party almost every Saturday night."

"Freddye will like that."

"You'll be included as soon as you meet a few people. Everyone is very friendly here."

"So far, I haven't had any free time. Even on the weekends I've been working."

I knew once Freddye came, we would both want to make friends and spend time with other Americans. Sure enough, when she joined me, we usually made plans every Saturday evening with other Americans. Often we'd get together on Sundays too, to explore as best we could within our 25-kilometer radius of permitted travel.

Much as we would have liked to socialize with the Soviets, *glasnost* hadn't moved society quite that far yet. There were laws still on the books that discouraged Soviets from spending time with foreigners. Memories of the consequences preyed heavy on most Soviets' minds.

Once we invited some of the staff to our apartment. Despite Freddye's efforts to make them comfortable, they sat fidgeting on the couch, reluctant to chat, afraid they might say or doing something wrong. Soon it was obvious they were waiting for just enough time to pass so that they could leave without being discourteous. We didn't invite them again because we didn't want to put them in an awkward position. We had a few parties in the office, which they all seemed to enjoy more. Freddye and I had a good laugh at one celebrating Christmas, New Year's, and Roman's birthday all at once, when Volodya mistook the coffeemaker filters for napkins as he set the table.

Corporate protocol required that any socializing I did with staff individually could only be with Vlasov. To put it bluntly, that would be awkward.

Once Roman surreptitiously invited me to his home so that I could see what a typical Soviet apartment looked like. We were out doing research at clinics for our Johnson & Johnson client. "I don't live very far from here. Why don't you drop by?" he said suddenly.

"Roman, are you sure it's okay?" We were actually breaking laws simply by going out on business alone together. Roman, of all the staff, was more willing to take risks, although with *glasnost* there wasn't much risk in simply making business calls with me.

"Gary, don't worry. It's fine. Please come to my home."

He led me to a typical, drab, badly maintained, gray apartment building. As we approached the door, Roman's wife ushered us into the E-shaped one-bedroom apartment. "*Vkhodi, vkhodi* — Come in, come in."

It became obvious that the two had planned my visit in advance because Irina had tea and cookies ready for us. On maternity leave from her job as a currency expert in the Ministry of Foreign Trade, Irina was delightful and spoke excellent English. "You'll have to stay until our baby wakes up," she pleaded with me.

We chatted for a while until we heard gurgling and giggling from the bedroom. I wished Freddye was with me because she would enjoy not only eighteen-month-old Sasha but the conversation with the Diukarevs, an intelligent and warm couple.

"I'd like for Freddye to come spend a day with me one day." Irina must have read my mind. Later, I told Roman, "I don't want to put you in any jeopardy."

"Let me worry about that, Gary," he assured me.

In the end, protocol—my job as CEO and his as an account director—and other circumstances limited Freddye and me from seeing the Diukarevs socially.

Outside of the staff, we found little opportunity to make friends with any Soviets. One exception was the head of our language school, who invited us to a typical Revolutionary Day dinner.

"Come and celebrate with our friends," Irena urged us.

Freddye and I wanted to go downtown to watch the parade that November 7 morning.

"It's really better on TV," Irena told us. "If you do go downtown, you have to get there before seven A.M. because they close off the streets and the Metro stops."

The parade didn't start until noon. So we would have to hang out in a coffeeshop for hours.

"Isn't the parade for the people? Why do they make it so difficult to get to?" Freddye asked.

"Well, not exactly. The parade's really for the people in the parade. Not for the spectators." We laughed, but Irena was dead serious.

"Self-aggrandizement," I whispered to Freddye.

So, like many in the rest of Moscow, we watched the November 7, 1989, Revolutionary Parade on TV, a much-reduced display of military force compared to previous years. For the first time ever, the government permitted demonstrators to parade and protest the lot of the Soviet people. I personally believe both parades were sponsored by Gorbachev and that he was using the counterparade to push those who didn't want to move as fast as he would like toward reform.

Later that evening we went to Irena's and met her husband and son and a German couple, who were also her students. She loaded the table with all kinds of food. She must have stood in line for hours and hours and hoarded food for weeks. Pickles, tomatoes, cucumbers—all carved into beautiful flowerlike shapes. The main course was pork in some kind of sauce. Meat is always a challenge because if it can be found, it's often a tough cut. The trick—so Freddye tells me—is to find a way to cook it for a long time to make it tender and still keep it tasty. But Irena's real coup was in finding some grapes. We ate them slowly, relishing every bite.

After dinner, we watched from her balcony as the whole city lit up in a beautiful coordinated display of fireworks. The sandstone buildings provided a superb background for the rapid bursts of light in blue, red, gold, and silver.

Since occasions like this were rare, the brunches at the embassy were our social lifeline. They were the times when even the various American constituencies attempted to mingle. The expat community was made up of State Department/military people, business people, and the journalists. For reasons I couldn't figure out, they never seemed to mix well. Considering there were fewer than five hundred Americans in Moscow, I found that puzzling.

Once I asked Rose Brady, the *BusinessWeek* correspondent, why it was, and she said, "I suppose different interests and the comfort level keep people from mingling."

One of the most relaxing, fun times I had was with Jeff

Trimble, the *U.S. News & World Report* correspondent. Richard Dean, one of our attorneys at Coudert Brothers, and his wife Susan, invited us to a picnic in the park one Sunday. Jeff and his family were also invited.

We carried baskets and blankets, Frisbees and footballs, all the things you take on a picnic, and found a shady spot to spread out. The kids ran off to play and we started unpacking the food. I noticed that we were being watched by groups of families.

"What's going on?" I asked Jeff, while peeking out the corner of my eye at the group gathering not too far from our blanket.

"They're just curious."

I didn't feel threatened but a bit uncomfortable, mostly because of the abundance of food that was not available to the Soviets. Jeff had been in Moscow for seven years.

"When I first arrived, you saw lines at stores only occasionally, not all the time like now," he recalled. "People weren't as willing to express their opinions, but they didn't seem as dissatisfied with their lives."

Even on purely social occasions like this one, we couldn't get away from talk about the overwhelming problems of this huge country. The posting for us Americans was difficult, though exciting. It was especially difficult for the spouses.

"Susan, you're a different person from the one who invited me to my first Moscow dinner last year," I reminded Richard Dean's wife.

The Deans' apartment was the first expat housing I had seen. Although beautifully appointed inside, it was in one of the international ghettos—a shabby old building, with a creaky elevator and dirty hallways. At the entrance to the parking lot a militiaman was stationed officially to protect the foreigners and their cars, in reality to keep an eye on their comings and goings and their visitors. That was my introduction to how expats generally lived in Moscow. Susan tried to put on a good face for newcomers, but her eyes couldn't hide her unhappiness with the tough living conditions. It was my first clue to what life would be like for Freddye.

"Yes, this is a better time for me now," she allowed.

Another journalist I came to know fairly well was ABC correspondent Rick Inderfurth. We had met before I came to Moscow at one of the Soviet seminars I attended, co-sponsored by Harvard and Columbia universities.

"We must get together when we're both there," we promised each other.

He moved before I did, but we made contact as soon as I was settled. Freddye and I enjoyed our evenings with these people and their families, all on this great adventure. We especially liked getting news from the journalists because they were often on the front lines—in Moldavia or the Baltic States, wherever there were riots or earthquakes or whatever—so they could give us the real scoop on what was happening. Local news was sketchy, unreliable, and often not available in English. I got most of my news by listening to the great BBC World Service on short-wave radio and devouring the magazines that came in my twice-weekly packages from Y&R in New York.

One journalist I admired and liked immensely was Quentin Peel, the *Financial Times*'s man in Moscow. He was a good friend of Mark Vecchio, another of our Coudert lawyers. Quentin was a small, wiry Irishman. He had lived in Moscow with his wife and numerous children (I think seven at last count) long enough to collect a marvelous repertoire of stories.

Since I often found the journalists as interesting as the business people—maybe because I studied journalism—I tried to bring the two groups together more, but I can't say that I succeeded.

Sometimes, the embassy's efforts as social planner failed miserably also. Once, soon after I came to Moscow, Mike and I were invited to a country-and-western night at the embassy.

"Sounds fun. Got anything better to do?" I asked Mike.

"No, let's go," he said.

We walked the few blocks to the embassy and passed by the Soviet sentry guard. When we came to where the American marine is usually stationed, he wasn't in the guardhouse and there was no one around to let us in. The administrative assistant at the embassy who invited us had said, "Call from downstairs and I'll tell the guard to let you in." But with no guard and no phone, we were blocked.

After a few minutes, a smartly dressed woman—her very high heels clicking sharply along the pavement—came up to the door, punched in the security code, and walked right in.

"Pssst!" Mike motioned to me to catch the door before it closed completely. I stuck out my foot to block it from latching, and we waited until she was out of sight and then entered. I couldn't believe that was all it took to break into the U.S. Embassy compound, and I felt kind of mischievous as we found our host's townhouse.

He wasn't too pleased either when we told him how we got in, especially since the embassy hadn't fully recovered yet from the scandal over the U.S. marines consorting with KGB women.

After a quick bite at his place, we went to the snack bar room where the country-and-western affair was going on. All we see as we enter is a guy with a boom box and a record player. That was it! There weren't more than five guys and even fewer women. Mostly good-ole boys, construction workers shipped in from Texas to work on the ill-fated, bugged embassy building.

We had a few beers, and some did a few rounds of the

Texas two-step. It was a fun evening, just getting out and meeting new people, though not what we expected, and certainly not the turnout that the embassy anticipated.

One of my proudest "insignificant" moments was when I became an official card-carrying member of the embassy. "Funny how such little things become important," I said to Mike as we were handed our cards. We couldn't become members until we had a business address, and that didn't happen until September 1989, almost a year after my first trip.

"It's great to be official."

"But everyone's been so gracious about inviting us as their guests," Mike reminded me.

"Still, great to have our own cards."

Mike and I started playing squash regularly. Mike was a fine athlete. He played football for ten years during high school and at Amherst, and won a National Football Foundation award. He was also proficient at soccer when he was young. The intervening years and his love of fine food had put a few extra pounds on his large frame, so, while he was technically the better player, I'd outlast him and would come on strong in the end.

During warm weather, sometimes a bunch of us would go to a park and lay out a softball diamond and play ball. That was great fun, too. Just the guys, our wives and kids. Our game attracted quite a bit of attention from the Soviets as they watched from a distance.

Once Freddye had arrived, Saturday nights were usually "our" night out for dinner at someone's apartment, or people would come to us. If they were lucky enough to get a movie or TV show from home, we'd all watch it together. Freddye and I also started up an informal exchange of tapes of TV shows and movies that friends sent in.

One especially enjoyable Saturday evening was spent at the Polishooks. Burt was the IBM exec in Moscow. "We managed to get a *Batman* tape," Burt said when he called to invite us. "And come for dinner at seven."

Moscow reminded us that good companionship is what makes for a great evening, not fancy entertainment and food. Our favorite business entertainment was the circus—a show where language makes no difference and everyone can relax. After a long workday, not everyone found opera, ballet, or drama in a language most of us didn't understand relaxing, and except for special guest performers and concerts, that was the extent of the selection. Once we went to the Bolshoi, but the ballet company, a pride of the country, traveled frequently.

Usually when the CEO of a foreign company visited—and there was a short period of several months when every American CEO with an office in Moscow seemed to want to come and visit—his company would organize a reception. Because the expat community was so small, you'd generally see all the same people there, plus the three or four Soviet ministers involved with the industries of the host company. If it was Dresser, then the oil and gas ministers would be invited. The American commercial attaché and even Ambassador Jack Matlock often attended. Matlock was very supportive of the American business community. Along with the same people, it was usually held at the same place—the National Hotel—because of the view of Red Square and because the traditional Russian meal was pretty good. Since we didn't have to deal with the desk clerks, the National Hotel wasn't too bad as a venue.

Sometimes, we'd hear about a new coop restaurant opening, and we'd usually get together a group of friends to try it out. Indian and Italian offered interesting changes in the routine. One of our favorite places was an old inn on the outskirts of Moscow, a rustic wood frame structure in a beautiful wooded area overlooking a river that froze solid in winter. I imagined it the perfect setting for a group of writers or artists, sitting at the heavy wooden tables debating the sad state of the economy and how to fix it. We'd usually go there on a Sunday, often after church services, which alternated between the American and British embassies.

The food was as good — or as bad — as any you got in town. You start with the same *zakuski:* pickled and salted smoked fishes, frequently sturgeon or herring, cheeses, pickles, olives, sometimes a pâté. Most times the main course was just served family style — meat in a thick sauce, whatever kind the restaurant could manage to buy that week. We dubbed it "mystery meat" because by the time it was cooked long enough to make it tender, you couldn't really tell what it was. Cabbage and kasha or potatoes were the most frequent accompaniments. This was a real bargain because they accepted rubles, and that made the meal very cheap — much less than $10 a person — at black market exchange rates.

When we got really desperate, we went to the Mercury in the Mezh. It was a very weak excuse for a supper club. The stage show was like a poor man's Las Vegas revue. The supper was worse. The waiter hands you an elaborate menu listing delicious-sounding French dishes.

"I'll take the veal Cordon bleu."

"Sorry, we don't have that."

"Then I'll have poached salmon."

"We're out of that also."

"Coq au vin, I guess."

"I'm so sorry. None either."

After going through that routine several times, I'd ask, "Well, what do you have?"

"Meat or fish."

The menu was a complete sham; but after a while in Moscow, any entertainment is welcome.

The night before we left Moscow for good, we discovered a not-so-bad nightclub, the Olymp. It was good enough that I wished I had known about it much earlier. Surprisingly, there were shapely women who must have been second string for the ballet because they didn't look like the typical stocky Soviet females you see on the street. The musicians were first rate also.

Often, it didn't take much to entertain us. Once Mike and I wandered into a nightclub, attracted by the sounds of the Creedence Clearwater Revival band. "Doesn't that take you back?" I turned to Mike.

"Just like any bar I remember from my Navy days," Mike reminisced.

"Same loud, raucous American-style rock music. And in such a non-American place." It was those little glimpses into Soviet life that made me stop and think about how much impact American culture and lifestyle had in most corners of the world, even penetrating a country as closed as the Soviet Union.

Freddye's move to Moscow helped me settle into a regular routine. I'd reach the office at about seven. Mike and I made a game out of who would get there first because the winner was rewarded by reading the telexes and faxes that came in overnight. Communication with the outside world was special.

Sometime between noon and 1:00 P.M., we left for a quick lunch, usually together—at my apartment when Freddye was home, and Mike's when she wasn't. The Soviets would have lunch after we returned.

Although official office hours ended at five o'clock, most

of the Soviet staff was still there when I left around seven. At first, I thought they stayed because they thought they shouldn't leave before Mike and me.

"I think they're staying because it's such a nice place," Mike said one day. "Better than their own drab apartments." Sure enough, after hours they would play games on the computers, or look at films or commercials that arrived in our care packages from New York.

During weekday evenings at home, if we didn't have any new tapes to watch, Freddye and I would listen to the BBC on short-wave radio to catch up on the news. And there might be an interesting play or music program on the BBC. On Saturdays, I'd stop by the office before going on to the embassy brunch. Mike and I frequently worked on client strategies during that quiet time. After the brunch, Freddye and I would shop every week for food at Stockman's or Sadko's, the two hard currency stores. We'd see many of the same people that we saw at the brunch earlier in the day. Then, if the weather was nice, we might go to a park, and later that evening to someone's apartment for dinner.

On Sundays, we'd usually attend church services. Sunday was also a day for sightseeing or spending time in the park shopping for artwork. Sometime during the day we'd usually clean the apartment. That took all of a half hour: Empty the wastebaskets, change the sheets, run the vacuum around, and dust.

A vacuum cleaner was another one of those precious pieces of equipment. We owned only one, which we used for the office, our apartment, and Mike's. If it happened to be in the wrong place, I was the one who usually carried it through the lobby of the Mezh. Sometimes, I was wearing my business suit, and I'd get awful strange stares. The staff was appalled that the CEO was hauling the vacuum cleaner, but no one volunteered for the job. I figured that was just another lesson about the West for them.

To take care of our clothing, Freddye usually took our laundry and cleaning to the hotel during the week; and until we were able to order a simple electric wash tub, she laundered the underwear by hand in the bathtub.

Moscow was not an easy city to call home. It took us longer to settle into a routine and hit our stride than in other cities we'd lived in; but eventually I felt comfortable with my life, both professionally and personally, in this tough town.

12

M Y   P A R T N E R

As I walked into my first orientation session on the Soviet Union, suggested by Alex Kroll in October shortly after I learned I was going to Moscow, I scanned the room for familiar faces: Jim Dowling, Mitch Kurz, Nick Rudd, Claire Montgomerie, Alex Kroll, John Cooper — all the members of the Soviet task force from either Y&R or Burson-Marsteller. My support group, my back-up resources and friends.

"Congratulations! Nice to know you're heading this venture." They patted me on the back or shook my hand. They were encouraging and complimentary, increasing the intensity of my excitement about the job.

I noticed some of them chatting with a tall, husky fellow toward the front of the room. He laughed a lot as they chatted, and I concluded that they must have known him because of the ease with which he seemed to join in the conversation. When I approached, they pulled me over.

"Here, Gary, meet your new partner. This is Mike Adams."

I had heard a bit about Mike through the agency grapevine. Mike was an associate creative director in Burson's Chicago office, removed enough both in geography and subsidiary so that we'd never met. Mike also was heading up Burson's Chicago crisis management unit. I figured between that training and my time on minesweepers in Vietnam, we were prepared for almost anything.

My instant reaction was that he was friendly and congenial. When I reached out to shake his hand, I stepped back a bit, realizing how much I had to look up. As I returned his firm grip, I thought, "This is a *big* guy. If nothing else, I've got a bodyguard if I need one."

Mike and I hit it off immediately. It didn't take long for us to find out that we shared, if nothing else, a love of sports and an enthusiasm for the job we'd been chosen to do. The following week we chatted several times on the phone between Chicago and New York as we prepared for our first trip to Moscow a week after the orientation. I grew very comfortable knowing that Mike would be my full-fledged partner in Moscow. I was the CEO, but knowing that Mike was my back-up and I could rely on him was comforting.

During the week, he filled me in a bit about his background. "This is my dream job," he confided. "I've longed for a chance to go back to Russia and use my Soviet studies."

Mike was a Soviet studies major at Amherst and had spent a summer in Moscow, Minsk, and Vilnius during college. He loved the history and language and culture. But as much as he tried, the closest he could get to using his knowledge of the Soviet Union was some international business assignments in Washington. Before he joined Burson in 1984, he worked at United Airlines and Amoco Oil. Much more realistic about the task before us, he understood the pitfalls we faced far better than I did.

I soon realized just how important our compatibility was. When our team arrived at the National Hotel in Moscow, we were tired from the long flight and the inevitable hassles. We all handed a disinterested clerk our passports and appropriate documents.

She checked her records, but obviously wasn't satisfied with what she saw and started looking at another set of records.

"Is there something wrong?" Mitch Kurz asked.

"Still checking," she answered curtly, without elaborating.

We engaged in idle talk as we waited for her to finish assigning our rooms.

"Well, guys, it looks like we'll have to make some adjustments," Mitch finally informed us. "They don't seem to have enough rooms. We're one short."

"Ask them to check again. There has to be a mistake," someone else from our party suggested.

"Look, we're in Moscow. Things don't work the same here." Mitch seemed quite prepared to accept the situation. "So let's just make do. Gary, would you and Mike mind sharing a room?"

"Fine with me," I said. "Okay with you, Mike?"

"Why not?"

We hauled our luggage to our rooms ourselves and struggled to open the door. As we entered the small, sparsely furnished room, I wondered if I had made a mistake in so generously agreeing to share a room. "I'll take the bed by the window. Okay?"

"Sure," Mike said.

I started thinking, "Is this a test to see if we can get along?" We'd have a week together in pretty close quarters. "Is Mike thinking the same thing?" I tossed my travel bag on the dresser and began unpacking as more questions ran through my mind.

Mike's thoughts obviously were wandering in a totally different direction, because the first thing he said to me even before he finished unpacking was, "Gary, it's been fourteen years since I was here. I've got to get out in the streets and see the people. Let's see who wants to go sightseeing."

Even though we'd flown all night, we were too excited to think of sleep. Several of us headed across the street toward Red Square and browsed in the GUM department store, where I got my first taste of empty shelves and poor-quality goods. Other stores had even less to offer. Nick Rudd took pictures of Mike and me in front of the famous St. Basil's Cathedral right in Red Square, and they later were published in *Ad Age* back home. When some of our group had had enough, Mike and I continued along Gorky Street alone.

"Everything has deteriorated so much. This isn't the same place I remember," Mike lamented.

Back in 1974, when Mike had visited Moscow before, it was a totally different era. Brezhnev was firmly ensconced in power, and life was better. There was food to buy on shelves and rubles were even worth something.

"Appalling, just appalling." Mike shook his head in despair.

"There wasn't so much gray back then. I remember color. Slogans and posters all throughout the streets and attached to sides of factories." He gestured toward the bare gray block buildings. "Banners announcing things like the Fourteenth Annual Anti-Capitalist, Anti-Imperialist Congress of the World. Maybe they were political messages like 'Forward, workers of the world,' or larger-than-life-size photos of Lenin, but they added color and interest to the drabness. Now there's simply nothing."

I could see that for myself.

Since the start of *glasnost*, the posters and banners had

been torn down; only a few remnants of the political propaganda remained. Thus far, there was no advertising to replace them.

Mike's wrenching personal reaction to conditions in the Soviet Union gave an added dimension to the cold and formal business negotiations of that week.

As days passed and negotiations progressed, Mike and I made more forays into the city. "It seems to me they're trying to embrace a capitalist system without any ethics," he concluded. "They want to assume the benefits of a free market in terms of the ability to earn and spend money and have material things, but the understanding of business ethics hasn't developed."

"We've certainly heard of a lot of 'they win–we lose' deals presented to us," I agreed, "and we haven't even been here a week."

The Soviets simply couldn't seem to grasp the concept that a deal is not a good deal unless it's win-win for all parties. Their attitude was, "If we win, that means you gotta lose." It was a tough week. The negotiations were difficult at times but also boring. My admiration and respect for Mike grew with each day that passed. He was tough when he had to be and compassionate at other times.

By the end of the week, I learned that Mike and I had much more in common than a love of sports and our determination to do a good job. I felt we were a good team, and if the hotel room situation was a test, we passed with flying colors — particularly the morning we both woke up with hangovers, each insisting the other use the bathroom first.

As we traveled back and forth over the next few months to press forward with the negotiations, Mike's understanding of the Russian psyche remained a big reason he could be optimistic and enthusiastic when depressing conditions dampened everyone else's spirits, including mine. It was those

times I especially appreciated his knowledge and a tempera-
ment that could cajole me into a more upbeat mood.

"I'd forgotten how black the imagery can be," he told me
after one somewhat troubling conversation with Vlasov and
Pashin.

We were riding in the car one day when Vlasov pointed to
a monument. "You know what that is?"

"Oh, yeah, the monument to the victory over Napoleon,"
Mike said.

"Well, you know that monument on the way to the airport? The one with the giant tank traps, that marks the forward progress of the Nazis?" We thought Vlasov was giving
us a history lesson.

"Oh, yeah, I know that one too," Mike said.

"Well, do you know the mistake that both those invaders
made?"

"What's that?"

"Well, they were both very capable in planning and exe-
cuting their entry into Russia and the Soviet Union. But you
know what they forgot? They both forgot how to leave."

Mike looked at me, and I wished I could read his mind. "Is
Vlasov saying the same thing about us? Are we a living
metaphor here?" I thought to myself.

As soon as we were alone, I asked Mike, "Was there some
sort of hidden meaning in all that? Was that a warning?"

Mike chuckled. "There's a lot of that kind of joking here.
With that kind of punch line. It's tinged with just enough
blackness that you can't ignore it. A lot of Russians believe
there's an inevitable course of Russian history, and foreigners
don't have any role to play."

"So what does that mean for us?"

Mike simply shrugged. I knew he didn't have a definitive
answer.

Those kinds of encounters didn't affect Mike as they did me, and if he had any reservations about our ability to succeed, he hid them. I could tell Mike was getting down when he declined to join me for a dinner we had planned or begged off from a squash date. I knew he was torn between his love of this job opportunity and the prospect that his wife and charming one-year-old daughter Katie wouldn't be joining him here. Mike and his wife eventually decided that it would be easier to have a commuting marriage. That was a decision that was sometimes reflected in the sadness in Mike's eyes.

Although Mike didn't discuss his feelings much, I knew that the lack of a traditional family life weighed heavily on his mind at times. He seemed to enjoy visiting Freddye and me at our apartment and sharing a meal; but he was careful not to be with us too much and wear out his welcome. As if he could.

The really fun times for Mike and me (if not for Freddye too) were when we got a Monday-night football tape from Alex Kroll via Express Mail. Freddye would make a special dinner, and after we ate, we'd make some popcorn and settle in for three great hours. Mike went through Amherst aspiring to a pro-football career and really knew the game, so he was our expert on-the-spot commentator.

Mike's relationship with the staff was different from mine. He was tougher on them, expected more and didn't excuse them from hard work because they lacked the tradition of an incentive/reward system. In one sense, when I was in Moscow, he was the odd man out, since I was responsible for most of the Western clients, and Vlasov and Pashin headed the Soviet ones. In another sense, he crossed over better from the Soviet to Western clients because he was the expert in public relations, and a much greater percentage of our business was in PR than in advertising. And, importantly, he was picking up his Russian again so fast that he could begin to conduct business in the local language.

Yet he still railed at what the rigid system had done to the people. One day we learned about a possible new assignment for Gevalia coffee, and we gathered the staff to brainstorm.

I was on one side of the table and Mike on the other, and we tossed out ideas and thoughts fast and furiously.

"Hey, this would be a perfect match with the space shuttle. What if we do this," Mike started out.

"Yea, but what if that happens . . . and this . . ."

After a few minutes, we realized the Soviets were sitting back in their chairs, their mouths agape, their heads switching back and forth from me to Mike as if they were watching a tennis match.

"Hey, guys, this is for all of us," Mike urged them on. "Give us your ideas."

But they just sat there, baffled. They couldn't figure out what we were doing. What did we expect of them? They were afraid they would say the wrong thing, despite our telling them that nothing they could say was "wrong."

"There's no right or wrong. We're trying to come up with all kinds of ideas. Then, we'll weed them out." Mike pressed them to participate.

But nothing we said could get them to open up. They did realize we were brainstorming, but they didn't feel comfortable proposing ideas that might be rejected, or worse, get them into trouble.

"The problem is," Mike told me after lunch, "that they

don't know how far they can go. They've lived under repression all their lives. Their motto is, If something's not expressly permitted, then it's forbidden."

Mike liked "informal" educational sessions, lounging in the office on a Friday afternoon with a beer. One day, Elena—who replaced Natalie as the receptionist when Natalie was promoted—asked if she could invite some of her friends to stop by. She was an attractive young woman in her early twenties, plugged into the music world.

Two of her folk music friends—bards in the true sense of the word—dropped in and gave a short concert. They were terrific and we were delighted. "If we ever do a commercial that needs your kind of music, you're it," Mike promised them. Bit by bit, we were treated to the talents that the Soviets were afraid to display for fear of some sort of repercussion.

During one informal get-together with the staff, we tried to impress upon them that all Americans aren't the same.

"You know," Mike explained, "Americans are as different as the Soviets. We probably have as many nationalities as you do. And I know that's a lot. What is it—scores? We just don't have the same concentrations. We reach across thousands of miles and have all kinds of different cultures, mixed together. Regionally, Bostonians are different from Hawaiians. We're not all like those hotshot New Yorkers that you think we are. And we're not even familiar with the wild, wild West that you probably see in the movies."

Mike could get very esoteric at times. He tried hard to convey that American values run strong and deep and that materialism doesn't pervade the whole of American society. He wasn't entirely successful, and sometimes his lectures went over the staff's heads, but much of what he had to teach was absorbed.

I guess you could say we too could be accused of pigeonholing everyone, and our general conclusion about the Soviets was that they're very conservative. One day, Mike called me into his office to see a startling presentation. A guy from the Soviet rock scene had come in to pitch us some business.

To digress a bit, when you're in Moscow, you have to do a lot of "kissing frogs." You have to see a lot of people you don't know about and don't expect to have any business with ever again because you never know when a prince is going to come by and jump on your lily pad. They walk in and say, "I've got an interesting sponsorship opportunity" or "an interesting media opportunity." In a developing market like the Soviet Union, you never can tell if the next Madonna or Steve Jobs will walk through the door, so it's in your best interest to listen to a lot of "frogs," despite the fact that it's very time-consuming.

Anyway, this man came into the office to show Mike some rock music videotapes that he wanted sponsored. Surprisingly, they were beyond MTV, far racier, more lewd and lascivious than anything that would have been shown on American TV. Here again it's the image of the racy American, and not the all-American boy, that is the Soviet perception.

Incredibly, this guy suggested, "Hey, don't you think Coca-Cola would jump at sponsoring something like this? This would give them a great rock image. Look, everybody's wearing black leather!" To make matters worse, the name of the program was "The Devil's Wheel."

"Have you ever heard of a company called Procter & Gamble?" Mike asked the promoter.

"Well, yeah, I know of them. Why?"

"Did you know they had a problem a couple of years back being accused of associating with devil worship?"

"Well, what does that have to do with anything we're talking about?" The guy was genuinely puzzled.

"The name of your program. American companies are very sensitive about things like that," Mike explained.

"But it's one of those carnival rides, like over in Gorky Park." He took a pencil and drew a picture of a Ferris wheel. "Why would that be a problem?"

Mike started to laugh because he realized that the literal translation into English is "devil's wheel." It was quite amusing.

But no matter. The show was still much too racy for any of our clients. So, we couldn't do much more than show him the door as politely as we knew how.

As serious as Mike was at times, he could be quite frivolous. At one staff meeting in a restaurant, he stood up and gave a speech, "I may be from the second city, but I don't take second place to anyone." At that, he tossed out knitted Chicago Bears caps to everyone and pulled them down over their heads. It was quite a sight. Here we were in a Japanese restaurant in Moscow with everyone at our table decked in American football regalia.

Mike was also a good host when we had guests in from out of town. Once when our Du Pont clients were in, he drove us all to dinner at the Delhi Indian cooperative restaurant. As was customary, Mike parked on the spacious sidewalk right in front of the restaurant. After a nice leisurely dinner, we came out, got into the car, and Mike started to pull away. We hadn't moved 100 yards before a street cop dressed in the typical long gray coat and big white gloves motioned for Mike to pull over. So Mike stopped. When the cop said something to him, he tried to play the old "don't understand" trick and responded, "Gee, I'd like to help you but I don't speak a word of Russian. Speak any English?"

The cop motioned for Mike to come over to his car. As he climbed in, the cop said, "You've been drinking, haven't you?"

Without thinking, Mike responded, *"Nyet,"* because he

knew how serious a drinking-and-driving charge is. Well, that blew his cover immediately.

The cop smiled and said, "Well, now that we have that straightened out, do you know what you did back there?"

"Nope, beats me," Mike said, no longer hiding his knowledge of the language.

"You parked on the wrong side of the street."

"What do you mean?"

"Don't you know about the new city regulation?"

"What new regulation?"

"The one that was passed today."

"How should I know about that?" Mike was getting totally exasperated.

"Everybody's supposed to know about it," the cop said smugly. "It says no parking on the odd side of the street because of snow removal."

I did notice a light dusting of snow on the sidewalk as we came out of the restaurant, but that was the first I'd heard of any decree relating to parking and snow.

"I haven't seen any newspapers or TV or listened to the radio," Mike told the cop indignantly.

"Well, ignorance is no excuse," he was quick to respond.

"All right, how much?" Mike knew the game.

Typically, while Moscow has a reputation for cracking down on drinking and driving, it has an uncommon system for moving violations for automobiles. If you agree to pay on the spot—guess where that money must go?—you don't have to appear before a judge. The cops are always incredibly polite but formal. They come up and salute you with a pleasant "Hello." They proceed to tell you what law you've violated, and their function is as much educational as punitive.

"So, how much?" Mike repeated.

"Ten rubles."

He settled up and we were on our way to take our guests back to their hotel.

As Mike drove toward the Inner Ring Road and approached the intersection we were looking for, he sighed. "Oh, no! I can't make a left turn here. We'll have to go all around." Left turns are very rare in Moscow.

It was late. We were all getting tired. "There's no one around. Come on, Mike. Just go ahead and turn."

"It's against my better judgment. I just got a ticket. What do you want from me?"

"Mike, the streets are deserted."

"Okay, here we go."

So he made an illegal left turn, and after about three miles delivered our clients to their hotel. I went to take them to their room and returned to find Mike deep in conversation with another cop parked next to our car.

"You know you made an illegal left-hand turn back there," I could understand that much from the conversation. "Show me your license and your papers and your car registration."

I knew Mike was livid.

"All right, Gary," Mike turned to me. "Break out your wallet. I won't say I told you so."

We sat there for the longest time as the cop gave Mike a lecture on how he shouldn't be driving in Moscow on an Illinois driver's license, and the rubles exchanged hands.

———

Sports were always a pleasant diversion for us. We'd shoot baskets at the embassy gym. Mike taught me to play squash, and we briefly got involved with American Trade Consortium representative Rick Spooner's Soviet baseball team.

One of Mike's favorite projects—so far all done on a volunteer basis—combined his love of sports with his desire to give the Soviets something Western. The Soviets are trying to establish a league for American-style football. Although they formed the league and named a president to get it moving, they had no idea where to go from there.

When Igor, the head of the league, came to Mike for advice, there were already about fourteen teams signed up, but Mike realized Igor needed some basic advice. For example, the teams were planning to play whenever two of them could agree on a free date. This most often would be on fairly short notice.

"That's not a good way to attract a lot of fans," Mike told Igor. "You need to form a schedule of games so that people can plan to come and watch."

"That makes good sense."

Other ideas such as seeking team sponsors, working with the media, promoting the league to build the gate were all new to Igor, and he welcomed Mike's suggestions. Mike's hope is that the league will catch on. Perhaps Y&R/Sovero can represent one of the teams on a paying basis.

———

I never worked as closely in my entire career with anyone as I did with Mike. We had a special relationship as we built the office together, both willing to put in the long hours required and put up with hardships neither of us had ever encountered before. Although our titles said otherwise, we worked as partners rather than boss and subordinate. After a while, we fit comfortably in each other's shoes and were virtually interchangeable: Mike taught me a lot about PR, and he picked up advertising from me.

When I left Moscow, I felt the office was in capable hands as Mike succeeded me. We had great laughs, frustrations, triumphs, and losses together. I'll miss his solid, good judgment, quick wit, and tenacious editing of my copy.

13

S A Y I N G G O O D B Y E

THE FIRST ANNIVERSARY OF MY INITIAL OCTOBER 1988 TRIP TO Moscow passed virtually unnoticed. When I realized that milestone had come and gone without any thought, I knew I had become a true expat once again. "Moscow's home now," I mused as I thought back over the events of the past year.

Like a college student who takes a couple of months to refer to a freshman dorm as "home," I had made it through the initial adjustment phase—a long one by most standards. Freddye had settled in, the success of our official opening was history, our daughters were managing in their new environments, Vlasov and I entered a period of relative detente. I found time for extra Russian lessons; going to the office across the lobby of the Mezh was becoming almost routine. You'd think my life was quite normal.

In some ways, it was. Take November 12, Freddye's birthday, a Sunday. We slept late and ate a leisurely breakfast, caught up on casual reading, and relaxed until the afternoon.

For dinner, we celebrated at a nice restaurant, a birthday celebration essentially no different than if we were in Westport.
The restaurant may not have had as many stars, but the occasion was just as special as the many we'd celebrated together
all over the world.

Yet, there was an uncertain edge to life here that kept you
on your toes. Freddye and I were still awaiting the arrival of
our multiple-entry visas. Every day we expected them to be
ready.

"Where are they?" I nudged our Soviet partners.

"Coming, coming," was always the response.

"They're absolutely a necessity," I kept reminding the
Soviets. "We're not going to stand for going through the hassle of applying for a visa every time we want to go and
come."

I continued to get the runaround.

"For some reason we may have to travel to the Soviet
Embassy in Belgium to get the visas," I warned Freddye.
"It'll be just a quick turnaround trip. That may be the only
way we're going to get them."

She sighed, accustomed by now to the red tape.

By the next evening, I was happy to report, "It's all taken
care of. Forget the trip."

More cartons of Marlboros and a makeup kit apparently
took care of the visas. Even though I'd been here more than a
year, I couldn't get used to the delays and the bureaucracy
and the graft.

"Mike, I feel like we're at the mercy of uncontrollable
events," I complained.

"It's been a tough week. Take it easy this weekend," Mike
said gently.

"The business of working here is exhausting. Is all this
effort going to be wasted because of the political chaos? Is all

this worth it?" Mike was my sounding board. We were working late. The Soviets had all gone home. As I looked out the window toward the Moscow River, I realized the shorter days, with so few hours of light between long stretches of darkness, were getting to me. Situated on a latitude similar to Edmonton, Alberta, far above the northernmost points in the contiguous forty-eight states, Moscow doesn't see daylight until well into the morning and darkness falls in mid-afternoon during the winter months.

"Gary, we have to go on. We can't give up now. Just think what would happen to all these people here if no one is willing to take any chances." Mike gestured toward the Kremlin, not visible from where we stood. He knew how deeply I believed in what I was doing. "We've got to have some faith that the leaders out there will find a way to improve everyone's lot."

I kept Mike's words in mind as Freddye and I remained glued more than usual during November to the BBC World Service network. "This is the best radio service there is, Freddye. I don't think I could live here without it."

The network was the most informative, entertaining, and balanced broadcasting anywhere. I've been a fan all over the world.

"It would be unthinkable not to have it, especially now," Freddye agreed.

It was from the BBC that we kept up with the astounding events that were now unfolding day by day in East Germany.

"To think that one of the most repressive, hard-line Communist regimes of all is the country where the barriers to democracy and the outside world are crashing down," I remarked to Freddye one evening as we listened to the account of what took place.

"And this is supposed to be the most successful Communist regime," she marveled. "It's incredible!"

Since the beginning of November, we had heard about the hundreds of thousands of East Germans storming their streets, demanding freedom and democracy. Others were trekking across the borders to Czechoslovakia—a door that had opened to the outside world. The democratic spirit began racing across the entire region. In Hungary, Parliament made moves toward ridding the country of communism. Czechs poured into Wenceslas Square in Prague to demand a new government. By the end of the month, it was clear that the Wall which had separated Berlin for more than thirty years was crumbling, and there was mention of a united Germany. All this in just a few short weeks.

And in Moscow?

"For once, there's no talk of anyone here acting to stop this avalanche of events," I said to Freddye one evening, gratified there was no intervention.

"Why do you think that is?"

"That's a tough question."

"Do you think it's because there are just too many problems here to worry about what's happening over there?" Freddye wondered.

"I wish I knew what they're saying these days behind those Kremlin walls," I admitted.

"Maybe Gorbachev has really wanted to encourage democracy all along."

"It's all so hard to figure out," I answered. "Politics is just not my forte. All I want to do is create the best ad agency in the Soviet Union!"

It was clear that the crumbling of the Wall which had represented such a clear division between two different worlds was a signal that the superpower that once dominated with an iron hand was open to other ideas. Unprecedented economic changes were taking place. The government has now taken a first step toward converting the ruble into hard currency. The "tourist" rate of exchange for the ruble has been dramatically improved in favor of foreigners to encourage travel and tourism. This is a good way to bring in much-needed hard currency. For so many years the government set an artificially high rate of about $1.60 per ruble. This made the cost of a trip in the Soviet Union as expensive as in any developed Western country, if not more so. For rates usually exceeding $100 per night, tourists get a dingy room and pay top prices for barely adequate meals. The new rate is 6 rubles per dollar—still a long way from the 20 or so rubles per dollar that can be found on the black market in Izmailova Park on the weekends, but a step in the right direction. For commercial purposes, we've seen no easing of the rate yet.

"Do you think changing the ruble is a direct result of all the changes west of here?" I asked Mike one day.

"Could be."

"Maybe this was planned a while ago?" I wondered.

"I suppose without the control over the economies in Eastern Europe, Gorbachev must realize that he's got to find other willing trading partners," Mike said. "It has to be difficult to wake up one day and realize that the status quo is just not going to work anymore. Who knows whether this is all part of a long-term plan."

I've never had to work before under so many uncertainties, so many unknowns. How do you develop a business plan under these conditions?

I knew Mike didn't have the answers, even though he was much more a student of the Soviet Union than I was. "The staff has a taste of the West through us. They sure seem to like it. I just hope we don't have to take away what we've been able to give them," he said.

"You know they're aware of what they've gotten into," I answered.

It was hard not to dwell on history in the making around us, even though we were so busy with our own work. During October we had operated in overdrive, putting the official office opening behind us and at the same time helping clients with the biggest-ever U.S. trade show.

November sped by. As Freddye and I prepared to go to the States for Thanksgiving, I had mixed emotions. "I can't wait to see the girls and our friends," I told Freddye one night as we were packing. "But there's so much to do here."

"We'll be back before you know it," she promised.

"Projects move along so much faster when Mike and I are here, especially now that the office is all set up and we can concentrate on client work. I'm anxious to keep up our momentum."

"There's plenty of time for that," she said. There was no way she could know that this was a false prophecy.

Despite the vast amount of work we had done in the space of a year—and a year that looked like it would end up profitably on the ruble side of the business—we had yet to run our first ad. I guess that was another first that I could claim, not so proudly—I was running an ad agency that hadn't run any ads after a year in business! That was to be our next major milestone. I was hoping that our first ads would be a public service campaign I had been working on for some time. It would give us some valuable exposure in the marketplace since we didn't have any product work yet.

We had asked for and received examples of Y&R's best public service ads from all over the world on drug abuse, alcohol abuse, child abuse, and AIDS. We screened them carefully to see which ones might work on Soviet television and were preparing to donate them to Gosteleradio. The network would donate the time. We would provide the spot free, with a credit line at the end that said: "This message brought to you by Y&R/Sovero and Gosteleradio."

"There does seem to be more advertising in Moscow than a year ago," I remarked during a staff meeting one day. "I wonder who's doing the work."

I was certain Western agencies weren't involved. The creative work was primitive and mostly for local enterprises. Typically, the ads were gray, with few photos and lots of copy. The production quality was poor, and the copy was dogmatic rather than captivating.

"Some of it reminds me of industrial advertising in the States in the fifties—lots of skimpily clad women selling equipment like forklifts and tractors," I said.

"It's a start," one of the staffers volunteered.

"That's true. I just wish we could get some of our ads on the air so people can see what's really possible in advertising."

The day came for us to leave for our Thanksgiving trip to the States. Often during that trip, my mind wandered back to Moscow. Especially so when one of my colleagues in the extended Y&R family, Tim Pollak, took me to lunch at Gallagher's Steak House in New York to encourage me to think about another job based in New York.

"Tim, I can't leave Moscow until my job is done," I protested. "I haven't accomplished nearly as much as I want to."

We celebrated Christmas with our girls on a skiing vacation in Italy. Somehow the bitter, nasty Moscow winter didn't seem as bitter or as nasty as it did the year before; the snow wasn't as dirty, the people not so grim. We continued to do good work for our growing blue-chip roster of clients: Kodak, Heinz, J&J, Colgate, Coke, United Airlines, Adidas, Xerox, Hoffmann-La Roche, Du Pont, General Electric, Rodale Press—a fine list of companies to work for. What other agency in the world could claim such a list in less than a year?

Then, in February 1990, I got a call from Alex Kroll. It was early morning New York time, but the end of our workday on a Friday. "I hate to make this call because I know how you feel about what you're doing—and because of how I feel about what you're doing," Alex started out.

He was offering me a new job—to succeed Tim Pollak as CEO of HDM, the seventeenth agency network in the world. I wanted to say no. It was not an easy decision to make. "It would be a great job that most people in advertising would kill for," I thought to myself. "How can I even hesitate?"

HDM was the Y&R joint venture with the Japanese ad agency Dentsu, an evolution of Alex Brody's old DYR that got a new name when a third partner, Havas of France, was added. The new name took a letter from each of the partners. Y&R chose to use the "M" from one of its subsidiary agencies called Marsteller to designate its ownership.

Tim saw me as his ticket out. But I had very mixed feelings. Running HDM, a $2.5 billion ad agency, was not a bad job. On the other hand, it would mean nonstop travel and that I would have to leave the city where the most exciting story of the last half of the twentieth century was taking place.

In the end I said yes. I knew my background was perfect for the job. I also felt that Freddye and the girls had given up a lot to support my great Russian adventure—probably more than I appreciated. By accepting the job, I could provide them with a more stable lifestyle.

Y&R/Sovero was up and running, with great prospects. We had done it, and it was time to move on. I was to become president of HDM on May 1—May Day, how ironic. It was like coming home—after four years in Japan, two in Paris, and eight years at Marsteller.

Y&R/Sovero did not stand still. The Soviets found another Chamber of Commerce veteran, Galina Kalinina, to replace Vlasov, who died on February 20. The staff complained that she would be even more rigid than Vlasov. Mike and I thought she seemed tough but efficient and fair. We hired her. In truth, we had no choice since she was nominated by the Chamber.

Our market research business continued to boom. We hired the first research director in the U.S.S.R., Natasha Ovchinnikova, a five-foot, 90-pound dynamo from the Institute for Sociology Research.

April 8, 1990: Our last Sunday. Freddye and I go for a walk to the Ukraine Hotel to buy souvenirs to take back. Moscow is as gray as ever. Spring has not shown any sign of arriving. Somehow, the Soviets out for their Sunday stroll don't seem so forbidding. I smile and nod as we pass and I think I see a hint of friendliness.

Back in the apartment, I look around our little home to see what's left to pack. I'm surprised at the few pieces of luggage that we have, packed mostly with clothes, some books, cameras. The furnishings will remain for Mike and all who follow from Y&R to take over my job and my apartment. At least they'll have much more of a headstart on comfortable accommodations than we did. We're leaving a big box of old clothes for distribution to the needy — the staff probably are too proud to take them, but I'm sure the clothes will disappear. I can't believe the depths of my sadness, a deep sense of loss. The staff are more like my family. I want them to continue to grow and learn and make better lives for themselves. Mike and I have given them a good foundation.

Tuesday: My last official day of business. We are holding our second board meeting. Jim Dowling and Alex Kroll cannot attend, but John Cooper represents Alex by proxy, and Seith Rothstein, our New York financial and business affairs manager, has made the trip and will vote Jim's proxy. Golanov and other members of the Chamber are present. During the morning, we go through the paces formally, reviewing the status of clients, announcing new business, discussing our capital spending needs, and giving the official stamp to hiring Galina.

Our business discussion continues over a long lunch, complete with typical Soviet vodka toasts and several courses of food and wine. Then Freddye and I go back to the office for our final goodbyes. The staff are all gathered in the conference room — Natalie, Pashin, Roman, Volodya, Fedorov, Elena, Mike — with mixed emotions as we come to yet another milestone.

Roman acts as a master of ceremonies of sorts as they proudly present us with a Russian tea service and a fancy ceramic plate with a painting of a bird. The plate symbolizes the first ad we ran to advertise the agency to international companies. The headline was: "The early bird gets the cherviac." As you probably guessed, *cherviac* means worm in Russian. More touching than their gifts are their kind words of appreciation.

Roman turns first to Freddye. "We'll miss you. You're our friend, our teacher, someone we could all turn to and count on. Natalie and Elena will especially miss you. You've been their sister, their role model, their inspiration."

When Roman turns to me, the tears are pouring down my cheeks. It is unusual that I cannot control my emotions. I give up trying to present a little speech I'd planned. Mike stands there grinning, a bit embarrassed. Everyone hugs. I take a good look around the office for one last time before Freddye and I go through the door.

During those final hours, I thought about the last year and a half and how I had packed in a lifetime of experiences and memories. Y&R/Sovero is certainly not the biggest office I've run from a financial standpoint, but it made the biggest impact on me. I will never forget the blossoming of Natalie, the steely blue eyes of Volodya, the proud, stiff Vlasov, the amiable Pashin, the bright independent Roman, and that great U.S. ally, Mike.

Moscow, too, had changed. The city we left was not the same one that greeted us eighteen months earlier. Perhaps nothing better summed up the changes than the crowds at two famous landmarks as we prepared to say goodbye: The line at McDonald's was now longer than the one at Lenin's tomb.

AFTERWORD: MOSCOW IS MORE THAN A MEMORY

MORE THAN TWO YEARS HAVE PASSED SINCE FREDDYE AND I SAID our final goodbyes to the Y&R/Sovero staff. My job since I left Moscow, running an American-Japanese joint venture ad agency, has taken me tens of thousands of miles from my New York headquarters, mostly to Asia and Australia. But somehow, despite my desire and good intentions, I have not been back to Moscow.

The political events that have occurred in what is no longer the Soviet Union are well known. I would have liked to have experienced the coup in August 1991 firsthand, but I must be satisfied by the stories of my partner, Mike Adams.

"Tell me more, Mike," is a familiar refrain when we get together. He tirelessly placates my craving for every minor detail about the goings-on whenever he gets back to the States or when I can reach him by phone early on a Sunday morning.

He tells me that when he woke up on that Monday morning in August and heard a Soviet broadcaster say that Gorbachev had stepped down for health reasons, he knew something else was up, so he flipped immediately to CNN for the real story. I'm not sure how much of the truth he heard even then.

Despite some apprehension about what was in store in the days ahead, he headed toward the office as usual and tried to conduct business, even though he didn't have full control over either his mind or his heart. Frankly, business did seem somewhat trivial, he tells me, when he thought of what might be happening.

"Is all of our work going to be worthless at the end of this week?" was the thought that he tried to put out of his mind.

Some of our clients, who didn't understand Russian or who did not receive CNN at home, recall that Monday morning quite differently. Unaware that anything unusual had occurred, they drove to their offices, surprised to see that rather than the usual rush-hour traffic, they were sandwiched among Russian tanks. Only later in the day were they aware that these tanks weren't out on routine maneuvers.

About half of the Y&R/Sovero staffers made their way to the office. They, too, tried to pretend it was business as usual. But as the events of the day unfolded and Mike went out to appointments, he couldn't get all the way back to the office in the car because of an almost carnival-like atmosphere in the nearby streets. Our office was quite near the Russian Parliament building, also called—seemingly ironically to an American—the White House. That was the building where Boris Yeltsin had taken refuge and was demanding the release of Gorbachev from the hardliners and his return. So, as Mike approached the office, he forged his way through the crowds on foot.

Many clients called and said they were getting out—on the

first plane, train, or any other transportation they could catch, because they were afraid they would be cut off from the rest of the world. Rumors were rampant: Gorbachev was being held in close quarters; he regretted what he had put the country through and was ready to repent; he was gravely ill; he was dead.

Mike said he had no fears, and in those tense early days spent hours faxing those in the West assuring concerned people—his family, office colleagues, and friends—that he was safe and didn't feel he was in a dangerous situation. "No, I'm not leaving," he repeated in faxes and in the rare instance he was able to get an international phone connection.

He and those staffers who did come to work kept themselves busy, alternating between watching CNN broadcasts and racing down the office corridor to the other end of the building where the Russian White House was in clear view from the thirteenth-floor windows.

There, tanks and crowds surrounded the Parliament building—some supporting the return of Gorbachev and others opposed. It was hard to tell whose side each group was on. Buses and trolley cars were turned on their sides to be used, if necessary, as makeshift bunkers, but for the most part the crowd, though nervously loud, was manageable. Little business was accomplished in the office, although Mike says he did complete one corporate image campaign. During this time, the embassy called on Mike to participate in a chain notifying Americans who didn't have phones (or phones that didn't work) of the State Department's official recommendations.

Meanwhile, clients were ordering their employees to leave on the first available transportation. Some execs who wanted to stay were ordered out, only to find that they couldn't buy a ticket for any price. In a word, it was chaos. One corporate exec was ordered to leave, alerted his wife, gathered up a few belongings, and as they started out the door toward the airport, answered the phone to learn that the order to leave was canceled.

Because Mike's apartment was so close to the Russian White House, he left his windows open at night so that he could hear immediately if a major assault was under way. He awoke several times to thuds and automatic weapon fire, but no major battle. The next day, he heard a report using taped scenes of that same weapon fire on CNN—sort of *Twilight Zone*, he said. Meanwhile, Mike kept assuring his wife and Y&R that as soon as he felt in danger, he would leave.

Every day, Mike told staffers that they shouldn't come in if they felt in any danger. Most days at least half the staff would show; on payday, the entire staff was in the office. Every day, Mike sent the staff home early. By Thursday, the intensity of the situation had abated and Gorbachev seemed to be back in control.

What would remain up in the air for some weeks to come was whether our clients—and other potential ones—would be willing to invest in this market as wholeheartedly as they had before. For a few months, they made decisions more cautiously, but they eventually came to realize that there is no turning back.

As Mike describes it, I'm not sure I would recognize life at Y&R/Sovero today. Y&R is even more in control because the American agency has taken a substantial additional equity stake in the joint venture. The Soviet partner has served its primary purpose of helping to gain influence and access under the old system. No one now even knows who the right person is to influence. Our Russian partner, the Chamber of Commerce, and its agency, Sovero, would rather have the hard currency Y&R paid than equal control of the joint venture, especially since equal control in ownership never really meant equal say in running the business. The buyout was made possible since Western companies are no longer limited to minority ownership.

That presents a whole new set of challenges for Mike. The office looks the same now but is going to move — to less expensive quarters, whose landlord accepts rubles. When I first went to Moscow, the official ruble rate was set at 1 ruble for $1.60. Now that same ruble brings only one penny. Despite the floating currency, which results in a more realistic rate of exchange, it's no longer practical to be so generous with our hard-earned hard currency. More deals are being conducted in rubles, and Mike must try to minimize his hard currency expenses in order to ensure profitability.

He has moved out of his Sovincenter apartment into Russian housing some miles away. His family may join him now that he has enough space to house not only his wife and daughter Katie, but also a new son born in the spring of 1992. There are reminders that this is still Moscow: his new apartment is generously larger, but has no kitchen as yet.

Mike will be joined by another expat, probably from Europe. Having a Y&R colleague is essential not only for moral support but to support the growing business.

The nature of the business has changed dramatically. I'm still somewhat chagrined that I left Moscow before we ran our first ad. It was only a few months after I left that Du Pont opened a plant and ran a magazine ad we created about a high-productivity herbicide. That may not sound very exciting to anyone accustomed to cinematic extravaganza, but it was a milestone that I regret missing. Since then, there have been TV commercials for Du Pont and Sony and others. And we did run posters on buses for Colgate.

Y&R's majority ownership means that Mike no longer has

to contend with a Russian counterpart. Galina, Vlasov's successor, proved to be much like her predecessor, but she is now gone, as are several of the original staffers.

Without the protection of Vlasov, Mike was finally able to get rid of Fedorov shortly after I left when he refused to report to Natalie on a project because she was a woman. Yuri, the accountant, is also gone. Mike's not quite sure of the real reason he decided to leave. Better-paying jobs obviously attract people who are desperate as the dropping value of the ruble raises the cost of daily life dramatically. Those who are trained in Western business practices and can speak English will be paid handsomely for their knowledge and training.

Loyalty? Does it have any meaning? I'm not sure. Mike is well aware that his best people—because they are so well trained—could be hired away by other Western companies willing to pay high salaries to get experienced Russians.

Pashin has blossomed as the senior Russian reporting directly to Mike, now that he has come out from under the thumb of an old-line Russian boss. Roman has continued to grow and is heading up the public relations group. Natalie, too, continues to grow in capability and confidence.

Y&R/Sovero no longer needs a driver because both Fords were totally destroyed when they collided while being driven back from Helsinki, where they were serviced. Roman and Volodya were uninjured. Mike commutes either on foot, by bike, or in his own Volga.

Y&R's original objective for starting up—to serve its clients entering this vast new market—was accomplished, although the American Trade Consortium never panned out. Nevertheless, Y&R has built an outpost to offer high-quality commercial communications counsel and services to clients, regardless of their agency affiliations in other countries. Although the agency is still young, it's considerably more mature than in my days in Moscow. Mike is guiding it on to the next stage of development, aiming to establish a superb creative capability. As the agency tries to raise its creative advertising profile, it still hopes to maintain its government and public relations services.

Today, the most active accounts include Johnson & Johnson, AT&T, Intel, Sony, and Colgate. Mike also sees some opportunities in the airline business and a new government lottery. He's spent hours trying to convince Yeltsin's people that the government needs to communicate its programs to the people, using Western marketing techniques to gain their support during such tough economic times.

A potential problem is the future of the media. The television networks, formerly fully funded by the government, are strapped for money and can't afford decent programming. Without good programming, they can't attract viewers, and without viewers, they can't attract advertising. Newspapers and magazines have reduced their frequency and size because they too no longer receive any government funding and can't afford to buy paper and other necessary supplies and services. The once mighty *Pravda,* that powerful voice of the Communist Party that published 8 million copies six days a week, stopped printing. *Izvestia,* the former official government newspaper, has a bit of newfound money in a publishing venture with the U.S. publishing company Hearst. The Tass news agency has resorted to trying to sell ad space on every square inch of building and lamppost in Red Square to make a few bucks. Only Lenin's tomb is off limits.

The events of the last few years in the former Soviet Union have allowed the world to see what Mike and I started glimpsing firsthand in the fall of 1988: a nation with the scientific capacity of a major nuclear power and space explorer, but whose people suffer the lifestyle of a Third World country.

Looking back, I realize that I entered the Soviet Union naively, totally ignorant of how much work was needed. Political freedom has taken a giant step forward; hopefully, economic freedoms will follow.

While I'd like my closing thoughts to be an inspiration for the future of the country, I'd be less than honest if I didn't express some of my deepest concerns.

Goods are starting to appear on the shelves; lines are shorter but now with the floating ruble and elimination of government price controls, people for the first time may not be able to afford goods even when they do find their way into the stores. Jobs are no longer guaranteed. The system was terribly bureaucratic and slow and has been removed, but there is not yet a new system in place, so no one knows who is in charge of directing forward progress. Who do you sign a deal with? And if you sign a deal with Ivan Isanovich one day, will Ivan be around tomorrow and have the authority to fulfill his part of the deal?

This is all part of the very difficult task of moving from a controlled economy to a free market economy—a much more difficult task than changing the politics. The key, I believe, is the convertible ruble, which will allow Western countries to come in, work, and take profits out. Jobs and quality goods will be created.

Will the country go back to communism? No. Although those days look good by comparison, the people understand that the old system delivered them into their present condition. Unfortunately, the Soviets must face many difficult years before they experience a healthy economy. It will require the help of the developed countries to train and teach as well as to give short-term monetary relief. Is this a wise investment? Certainly it is, for business reasons as well as humanitarian ones.